까칠한

Grammar

감성 맞춤 내신 공략

길들이기

까칠한 GRAMMAR 길들이기 마무리 1

출판일 　|1판 1쇄 발행 2014년 10월 30일

지은이 　|박설희, 김일선
펴낸이 　|최회영
책임편집 |김소연, 이수미
영문교열 |이윤선, 윤은지, 강소영, J. M. Ferguson
디자인 　|노영남, 이보람
펴낸곳 　|(주)컴퍼스미디어
출판신고 |1980년 3월 29일 제 406-2007-00046 © ㈜ 웅진씽크빅 2011
주소 　　|서울특별시 서초구 서초2동 1360-31 정진빌딩 3층
전화 　　|(02)3471- 0096
홈페이지 |http://www.compasspub.com
ISBN 　　|978-89-6697-834-2

이 책의 구성과 특징

01

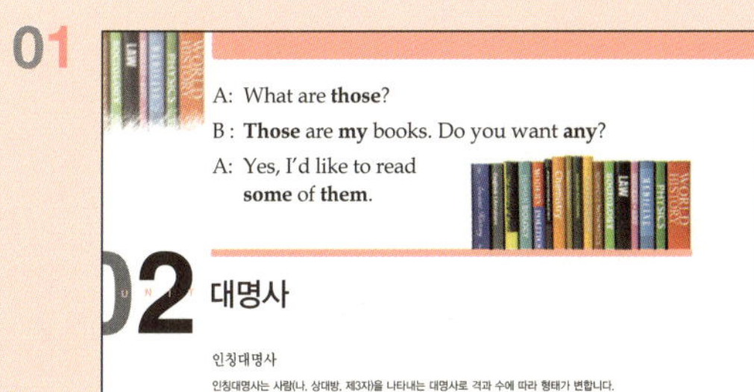

Introduction

각 unit의 대표 문법이 다양한 상황 안에서 사용된 내용을 사진과 함께 미리 제시함으로써 관련 내용의 개요를 활성화하여 학습에 대한 흥미를 높일 수 있도록 하였습니다. 대화문, 담화문, 수수께끼 등을 이용한 학습의 시작은 학생들의 집중도를 높이고, 학습에 대한 부담감을 줄여줄 수 있습니다.

02

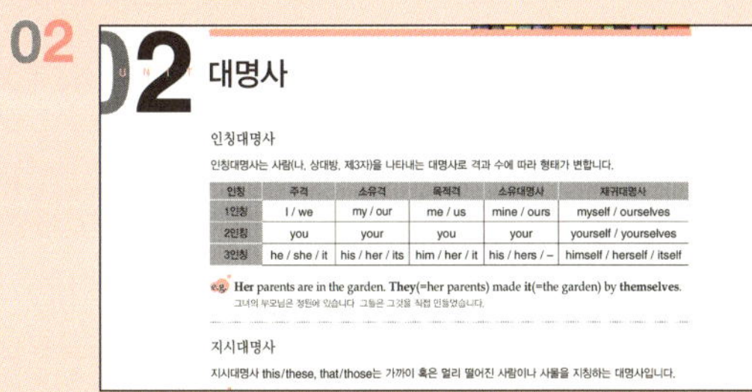

Easy Explanation and Plenty of Examples

알기 쉽게 정리된 설명과 적절한 예문을 제공하여 중등 영문법 기본 실력을 튼튼히 다질 수 있습니다.

03

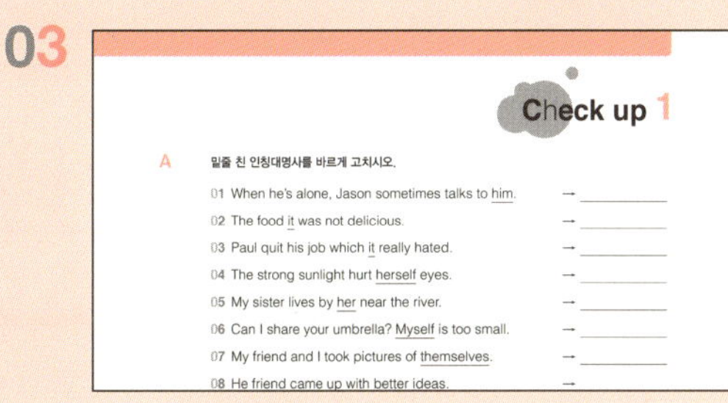

Check Up

Check up 1에서는 비교적 쉽고 간단한 유형의 문제를, Check up 2에서는 좀더 심화된 내용의 문제를 풀어보면서 해당 Unit에서 배운 문법을 얼마나 잘 이해하고 있는지 점검해 볼 수 있습니다.

04

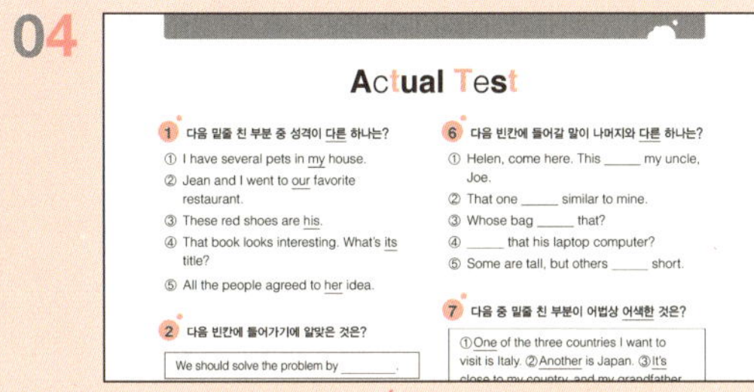

Actual Test

배운 문법을 내신 시험에 적용하여 바로 풀어볼 수 있도록 10개의 문제를 제시하였습니다. 이로써 학생들은 해당 문법이 학교 시험에서는 어떠한 형태로 출제되는지 미리 알고 실전 감각을 기를 수 있습니다. 10문제 중 3문제는 서술형으로 출제하여 실제 시험과의 연관성을 높이고 서술형 평가에 효과적으로 대비할 수 있게 하였습니다.

05

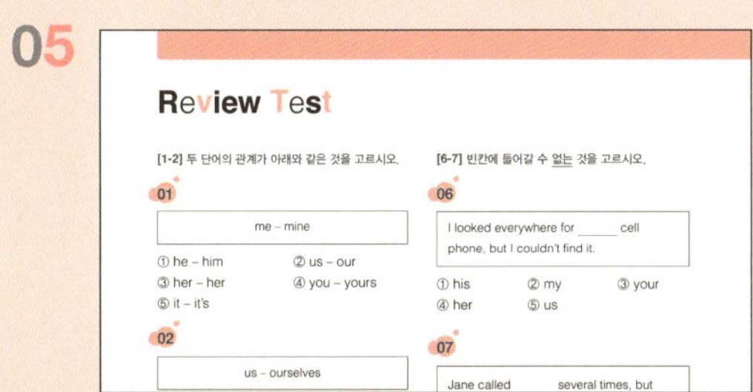

Review Test

각 Chapter의 학습이 끝난 후, 배운 내용을 종합하여 평가하고 점검할 수 있도록 Review Test를 구성하였습니다.

Table of Contents

명사와 대명사

01 명사의 종류　02 대명사

I drink **a glass of milk** in the morning.
I eat some boiled **eggs**, too.
They are all from **Uncle Kevin**'s
farm house.

01 명사의 종류

일반명사 (가산명사와 불가산명사)

사람·동물·사물을 두루 가리키는 명사로, 가산명사(셀 수 있는 명사)와 불가산명사(셀 수 없는 명사)로 나뉩니다.

	정의	복수형	부정관사 a/an	정관사 the
가산명사	일정한 형태를 갖추고 있어 수를 셀 수 있음 (cup)	O (cups)	O (a cup)	O (the cup)
불가산명사	형태가 없는 물질이나 추상적 개념을 가리킴 (water)	X (−)	X (−)	O (the water)

e.g. 가산명사: teacher, nurse, lion, museum, computer, building, hour, dollar, meter 등
불가산명사: coffee, wood, glass, ice, bread, meat, air, smoke, sand, sugar, salt 등
(불가산명사의 수량은 단위명사로 나타냄: **a cup of** milk, **two glasses of** water 등)

고유명사

인명이나 지명 같은 고유의 대상을 가리키기 때문에 복수형을 만들 수 없습니다. 항상 첫 글자는 대문자로 쓰며, 아래의 경우를 제외하고는 기본적으로 관사를 붙이지 않습니다.

고유명사	Michael Jackson, Asia, Australia, London, Mt. Everest, Monday, January 등
the + 고유명사	신문, 공공건물, 선박 등: The New York Times, the White House, the British Museum, the Mayflower
	강, 바다, 산맥: the Pacific Ocean, the Red Sea, the Han River, the Rocky Mountains, the Great Lakes
	나라 이름(단수취급): the United States, the Netherlands, the Philippines

추상명사

구체적 사물이나 사람이 아닌 추상적인 개념을 나타내는 명사로, 셀 수 없으며 단수 취급합니다.

e.g. life(인생), hope(희망), art(예술), beauty(아름다움), advice(조언), weather(날씨) 등
Life is beautiful. 인생은 아름답다.　　It's really good **advice**. 그건 참 좋은 조언이야.

Check up 1

A 괄호 안에서 알맞은 것을 고르시오.

01 My mom gave me (an umbrella, umbrella) in the morning.

02 Jerry wants a new (computer, computers).

03 Do you have some cold (water, waters)?

04 We need (wood, woods) to make a table.

05 I need two (hour, hours) to finish my homework.

06 Where is (a smoke, the smoke) coming from?

07 These earrings are made of (gold, a gold).

08 There are some (bread, breads) and milk left.

09 The new pen costs two (dollar, dollars).

10 Please pass me (a salt, the salt) on the table.

B 고유명사에 동그라미 하고 필요한 경우 빈칸에 the를 쓰시오.

01 Tom lives in ________ United States.

02 It's ________ Sunday today.

03 I want to go to ________ China.

04 Do you know ________ Ms. Smith?

05 ________ White House is where the U.S. president lives.

06 ________ Seoul is the capital of my country.

07 Where is ________ Pacific Ocean on this globe?

08 ________ *New York Times* is a newspaper company.

09 Ted is planning to climb ________ Mt. Everest this winter.

10 Have you ever been to ________ Europe?

A 다음 그림을 보고 알맞은 단어를 골라 문장을 완성하시오.

01   02   03   04   05

| beauty | hope | weather | advice | art |

01 My grandma always gives me good ___________.

02 Sarah is famous for her ___________.

03 I don't have any ___________ of finding my wallet.

04 Most people hate rainy ___________.

05 Galleries have famous works of ___________.

B 다음을 읽고 밑줄 친 부분을 바르게 고치시오.

I went shopping last **01** sunday. On my way to the department store, I met **02** janice. She wanted to buy some **03** book about **04** the Japan because she was planning to go there. I needed to buy two bottles of **05** milks and some **06** breads, too. So we went to the store together. She bought a book with a lot of tourist **07** informations. After shopping, we drank **08** juices and went back home. I had a good **09** times with her.

01 _______________   **02** _______________   **03** _______________

04 _______________   **05** _______________   **06** _______________

07 _______________   **08** _______________   **09** _______________

Actual Test

1 다음 빈칸에 들어가기에 알맞은 것은?

> The building is 10 __________ long.

① meter ② a meter ③ meters
④ the meter ⑤ the meters

2 다음 중 빈칸에 a(n)이 들어갈 수 <u>없는</u> 것은?

① I'd like to buy ______ laptop computer.
② The ice cream is just ______ dollar.
③ There is ______ parrot in the cage.
④ My cat likes ______ small ball.
⑤ We cannot breathe without ______ air.

[3-4] 다음 밑줄 친 부분 중 어법상 어색한 것은?

3 Mr. <u>Smith</u> always <u>gives</u> me good
① ②
<u>advices</u> about <u>my</u> school <u>life</u>.
③ ④ ⑤

4 We need two <u>cups</u> of <u>milk</u>, <u>butters</u>,
① ② ③
<u>sugar</u> and flour to make <u>a cake</u>.
④ ⑤

5 다음 빈칸에 들어갈 말이 바르게 짝지어진 것은?

> • There are many islands in __(A)__ Pacific Ocean.
> • She has __(B)__ daughter and two sons.

① the – a ② the – the ③ the – an
④ a – the ⑤ a – a

6 다음 중 어법상 <u>어색한</u> 문장은?

① Ji-sung Park is my favorite football player.
② She doesn't like sugar in her coffee.
③ I like the feeling of sand beneath my feet.
④ The London is the capital of the U.K.
⑤ I've never visited museums in Seoul.

7 다음 중 어법상 <u>어색한</u> 것은?

> Ted, please buy these things at the market for me, will you?
>
> · A bottle of ①<u>water</u> (big one)
> · Two loaves of ②<u>bread</u>
> · A box of ③<u>cookies</u>
> · Two egg ④<u>sandwiches</u>
> 　　　30 ⑤<u>dollar</u> in total
>
> 　　　　　　　　　　　　From Mom

[8-9] 밑줄 친 부분 중 틀린 것 두 개를 찾아 바르게 고치시오.

> How do you spend your ①<u>weekend</u>?
> I usually ride my ②<u>bicycle</u> to ③<u>Han River</u>
> and take a rest there. After riding my
> bicycle, I drink a lot of ④<u>waters</u> because
> I feel very thirsty. When ⑤<u>the weather</u> is
> bad, I just stay at home and read a book.

8 __________ → __________

9 __________ → __________

10 주어진 단어들을 배열하여 문장을 완성하시오.

(you / a / can see / tigers / two / here / lion and)

→ __________

A: What are **those**?

B : **Those** are **my** books. Do you want **any**?

A: Yes, I'd like to read **some** of **them**.

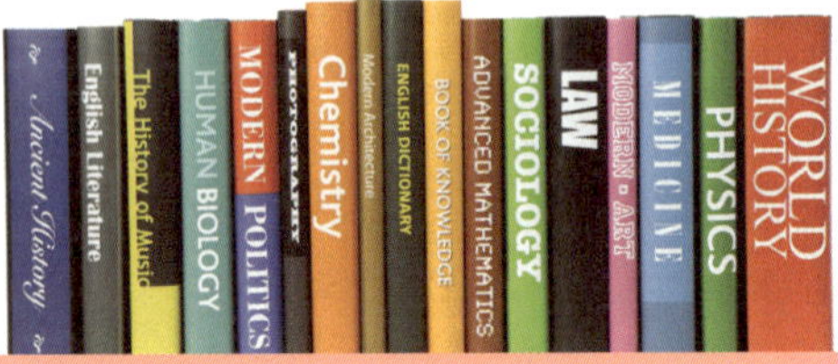

02 대명사

인칭대명사

인칭대명사는 사람(나, 상대방, 제3자)을 나타내는 대명사로 격과 수에 따라 형태가 변합니다.

인칭	주격	소유격	목적격	소유대명사	재귀대명사
1인칭	I / we	my / our	me / us	mine / ours	myself / ourselves
2인칭	you	your	you	your	yourself / yourselves
3인칭	he / she / it	his / her / its	him / her / it	his / hers / –	himself / herself / itself

e.g. **Her** parents are in the garden. **They**(=her parents) made **it**(=the garden) by **themselves**.
그녀의 부모님은 정원에 있습니다. 그들은 그것을 직접 만들었습니다.

지시대명사

지시대명사 this/these, that/those는 가까이 혹은 멀리 떨어진 사람이나 사물을 지칭하는 대명사입니다.

e.g. Is **that** your eraser?/ Are **those** your friends? 저것은 네 지우개니? / 저 애들은 네 친구니?
Sarah knew his birthday. **That**(= Sarah knew his birthday) made him very happy.
Sarah는 그의 생일을 알고 있었다. 그것이 그를 매우 기쁘게 했다.

Take **this** ball in my hand. (지시형용사) 내 손에 있는 이 공을 뺏어 봐.

부정대명사

지시대명사가 특정한 것을 가리키는 반면, 부정대명사는 불특정한 사람·사물 등을 가리킵니다.

one	another	the other(s)	some	others
• 앞에 나온 명사를 대신함 (복수 ones) • 정해진 수 중 처음 언급한 하나	• 앞에 나온 명사와 같은 종류이나 다른 것 • 정해진 수 중 다른 하나를 지칭	• 정해진 수 중 마지막 남은 하나 또는 여럿	불특정한 일부	또 다른 일부

e.g. There are three animals. **One** is a cat, **another** is a dog, and **the other** is a hamster.
세 마리의 동물이 있다. 하나는 고양이, 다른 하나는 개, 나머지 하나는 햄스터이다.

Some books are fun, but **others** are not. 어떤 책들은 재미있고, 다른 것들은 재미없다.

Check up 1

A　밑줄 친 인칭대명사를 바르게 고치시오.

01　When he's alone, Jason sometimes talks to <u>him</u>.　→ ______________

02　The food <u>it</u> was not delicious.　→ ______________

03　Paul quit his job which <u>it</u> really hated.　→ ______________

04　The strong sunlight hurt <u>herself</u> eyes.　→ ______________

05　My sister lives by <u>her</u> near the river.　→ ______________

06　Can I share your umbrella? <u>Myself</u> is too small.　→ ______________

07　My friend and I took pictures of <u>themselves</u>.　→ ______________

08　<u>He</u> friend came up with better ideas.　→ ______________

09　The manager gave money to <u>his</u> yesterday.　→ ______________

10　Our teacher promised <u>our</u> to end the class early.　→ ______________

B　괄호 안에서 알맞은 대명사를 고르시오.

01　Come here, and have some cookies. I made (these, this) by myself.

02　Who's the woman standing over there? – (That, This) is my cousin.

03　Do you have any books about cats? I'd like to read (one, it).

04　Beth told bad stories about me. (Those, That) made me very angry.

05　(Some, Any) of the travelers are from Japan.

06　Some girls like to play inside, but (the other, others) don't.

07　I have three brothers. One is taller than me, and (others, the others) are shorter than me.

08　Do you have a red pen? – Yes, I have (it, one).

09　Jenny has two cousins. One lives in the city, and (another, the other) lives on a farm.

10　The store sells two kinds of fruit. One is melons, and (another, the other) is cherries.

Check up 2

A 다음 표를 보고 빈칸에 알맞은 대명사를 쓰시오.

My best friend Jerry and I

	Birthday	Family	Hobby	Pet
Jerry	February 28th, 1998	parents, three brothers	playing the guitar	a cat
I	August 12th, 1999	parents, no siblings	doing yoga	two dogs

01 Jerry is my best friend. _________ birthday is February 28th.

02 My birthday is in August, so Jerry is one year older than _________.

03 Jerry has brothers. But I don't have _________.

04 Jerry has three brothers. One is older than me, and the _________ are
    younger than me.

05 Jerry plays the guitar almost every day. That makes _________ happy.

06 I like doing yoga. _________ is good for my health.

07 There are five people in Jerry's family except him. Two are parents,
    and _________ are all his brothers.

08 I have two pet dogs. One is white, and the _________ is black.

B 주어진 대명사를 알맞은 형태로 바꾸어 글을 완성하시오.

Penguins are interesting animals. I think 01 _________(they) are very
cute, so I chose 02 _________(they) for 03 _________(I) science project.
04 _________(they) are birds, but they cannot fly 05 __________(they).
Millions of years ago, they had wings. However, 06 _________(this)
became useless because they didn't have to fly much. The penguin
eats fish. 07 _________(it) lives in water, so the wings became flippers.
08 _________(it) ability to fly wasn't needed anymore. When I go to a zoo
by 09 _________(I), I always spend some time watching penguins walk.
10 _________(that) makes me smile every time.

Actual Test

1 다음 밑줄 친 부분 중 성격이 다른 하나는?

① I have several pets in <u>my</u> house.
② Jean and I went to <u>our</u> favorite restaurant.
③ These red shoes are <u>his</u>.
④ That book looks interesting. What's <u>its</u> title?
⑤ All the people agreed to <u>her</u> idea.

2 다음 빈칸에 들어가기에 알맞은 것은?

> We should solve the problem by __________.

① myself   ② yourself   ③ yourselves
④ ourselves   ⑤ themselves

3 다음 빈칸에 들어갈 말이 바르게 짝지어진 것은?

> • She called __(A)__ after she heard the news.
> • He had no idea about __(B)__ problems.

① he – her
② him – her
③ his – himself
④ his – her
⑤ himself – hers

[4-5] 다음 밑줄 친 부분 중 어법상 어색한 것은?

4 <u>All</u> of you <u>did a</u> good job. <u>You</u> should
　①　　　　②　　　　③
be <u>proud</u> of <u>yourself</u>.
　④　　　⑤

5 I got <u>two</u> letters from my family. <u>One</u>
　　　①　　　　　　　　　②
was from <u>my</u> father, and <u>another</u> was from
　　　③　　　　　　④
<u>my</u> brother.
⑤

6 다음 빈칸에 들어갈 말이 나머지와 다른 하나는?

① Helen, come here. This ______ my uncle, Joe.
② That one ______ similar to mine.
③ Whose bag ______ that?
④ ______ that his laptop computer?
⑤ Some are tall, but others ______ short.

7 다음 중 밑줄 친 부분이 어법상 어색한 것은?

> ①<u>One</u> of the three countries I want to visit is Italy. ②<u>Another</u> is Japan. ③<u>It's</u> close to my country, and my grandfather lives there. I want to go there to meet him. ④<u>Another</u> is China. I want to see the Great Wall ⑤<u>myself</u>.

[8-9] 주어진 단어들을 배열하여 문장을 완성하시오.

8 (she / looking at / is / herself)

→ ________________________ in the mirror.

9 (favorite doughnuts / my / are / these)

→ Come here and have some. __________

____

10 그림을 보고, 밑줄 친 부분을 바르게 고치시오.

A: Who's the girl with a big bag?
B: <u>This is Sarah</u>, one of my best friends.

→ ________________________

Review Test

[1-2] 두 단어의 관계가 아래와 같은 것을 고르시오.

01 

me – mine

① he – him   ② us – our
③ her – her   ④ you – yours
⑤ it – it's

02

us – ourselves

① we – our   ② he – himself
③ they – themselves   ④ she – herself
⑤ you – yourselves

[3-5] 다음 밑줄 친 명사와 그 종류가 <u>다른</u> 하나는?

03

Monica is my favorite <u>friend</u>.

① animal   ② doll   ③ book
④ advice   ⑤ piano

04

Do you have any <u>information</u> about our new teacher?

① happiness   ② thoughts   ③ building
④ hope   ⑤ concerns

05

I would like to have some <u>juice</u>.

① meter   ② wood   ③ sugar
④ meat   ⑤ ice

[6-7] 빈칸에 들어갈 수 <u>없는</u> 것을 고르시오.

06

I looked everywhere for _______ cell phone, but I couldn't find it.

① his   ② my   ③ your
④ her   ⑤ us

07

Jane called _______ several times, but there was no answer.

① them   ② him   ③ us
④ yours   ⑤ her

[8-9] 다음 중 어법상 <u>틀린</u> 문장을 고르시오.

08 

① Smoking is bad for your health.
② Would you pass me the salt?
③ He ordered some meat.
④ Please have this fresh loaf of bread.
⑤ She drinks cup of coffee every day.

09

① I've never been to the Netherlands.
② The United States are in North America.
③ The Red Sea is in the Middle East.
④ It's usually cold in March here.
⑤ The ship sailed across the Indian Ocean.

10

① It's too hot, and I need some air.

② It takes two hour to get to the station.

③ I wanted some breads for lunch.

④ A good advice might sound bad.

⑤ There are many people near a Han River.

11

① That people look very tired.

② Are these their travel plan?

③ Those red one looks nice.

④ I have any good news for you.

⑤ Some hate rainy days, but others don't.

12 다음 빈칸에 들어갈 말이 바르게 짝지어진 것은?

> **A:** Who lives in _____(A)_____ White House?
>
> **B:** The president of _____(B)_____ United States lives there. It's a very nice place.

① ø – the   ② the – the   ③ a – the

④ the – ø   ⑤ ø – ø

* ø = 관사 없음

[13-14] 빈칸에 공통으로 들어가기에 알맞은 것을 고르시오.

13

> • We made all the food _______.
>
> • Paul and I were traveling by _______.

① myself   ② yourself   ③ yourselves

④ themselves   ⑤ ourselves

14

> • Look over there. Is _____ what you're looking for?
>
> • What is _____ on his ear? Is it an earring?

① this   ② that   ③ one

④ some   ⑤ any

[15-16] 밑줄 친 부분의 성격이 나머지와 다른 하나를 고르시오.

15

① Can you lend me one <u>dollar</u>?

② Mr. Garrison is my English <u>teacher</u>.

③ I don't have any <u>advice</u> for you.

④ Have you visited an art <u>museum</u>?

⑤ The <u>building</u> is the tallest in my town.

16

① He hasn't been to <u>his</u> new house yet.

② I don't know any of <u>their</u> names.

③ She didn't read <u>your</u> letters.

④ <u>Our</u> plan was changed to a new one.

⑤ The red shoes over there are <u>hers</u>.

[17-18] 주어진 단어들을 바르게 배열하시오.

17 (milk / me / a / of / gave / cup)

→ She ___________________________.

18 (and / red / is / the / one / other)

→ I have two colored pencils: ___________
___________________ is blue.

[19-20] 주어진 우리말을 영어로 알맞게 옮긴 것을 고르시오.

19

행복은 작은 것들에서 온다.

① A happiness comes from small thing.
② A happiness comes from small things.
③ The happiness comes from small thing.
④ Happiness comes from small thing.
⑤ Happiness comes from small things.

20

그 책 자체는 재미없었다.

① The book themselves were not fun.
② The book by itself was not fun.
③ The book yourself was not fun.
④ The book itself was not fun.
⑤ Itself the book was not fun.

[21-22] 어법상 <u>어색한</u> 부분을 찾아 바르게 고치시오.

21 ___________ → ___________

I only know about one of these three books.
Do you have any idea about others?

22 ___________ → ___________

We don't have red shoes, but you could
have blue one instead.

[23-24] 다음 글을 읽고 물음에 답하시오.

American football is a very popular game
in ①the United State. ②It was invented
at colleges in the late 1800s from two
different ③games. ___(A)___ are soccer
and rugby. Football is similar to soccer in
that ④you can move the ball by kicking
___(B)___. Football is also similar to rugby
in that you can run with the ball and tackle
⑤the player who has the ball.

23 위 글의 밑줄 친 부분 중 어법상 <u>어색한</u> 것은?

①　　②　　③　　④　　⑤

24 위 글의 (A), (B)에 들어갈 대명사를 쓰시오.

(A) ___________　　(B) ___________

동사의 시제

It **rained** a lot yesterday.

In this region, it **usually rains** a lot in summer.

It **will rain** a lot this weekend, too.

03 단순시제

현재 시제

현재 시제는 현재의 상태나 감정, 일반적 사실, 습관 또는 반복되는 일, 일정이나 정해진 스케줄, 불변의 진리를 나타냅니다. be동사는 주어에 따라 **am, are, is** 로 바뀌며, 일반동사는 3인칭 단수 주어가 올 경우에만 뒤에 -(e)s가 붙습니다.

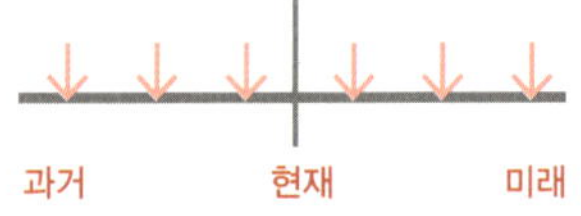

e.g. Peter **is** sick, so he **is** in bed now. Peter는 아파서 지금 침대에 있다.

Tom usually **wakes** up at 7 o'clock in the morning. Tom은 대부분 아침 정각 7시에 일어난다.

I **visit** my grandma on weekends. 나는 주말마다 할머니를 찾아 뵙는다.

Hot air **goes** up, and cool air **goes** down. 뜨거운 공기는 올라가고 차가운 공기는 내려간다.

과거 시제

과거 시제는 특정 과거 시점에 일어난 일이나 역사적 사실을 나타내며, 주로 과거 시간을 나타내는 부사어와 함께 쓰입니다. be동사는 주어에 따라 **was, were**로 바뀌며, 일반동사는 뒤에 -(e)d가 붙거나 불규칙 과거형이 쓰입니다.

e.g. **Were** you out of town last weekend? 너는 지난 주말에 시내 밖에 있었니?

She **told** me that it **snowed** a lot yesterday. 그녀는 나에게 어제 눈이 많이 왔다고 말해 주었다.

Dad **didn't know** how to send text messages before. 아빠는 전에 문자 메시지를 보내는 법을 모르셨다.

미래 시제

미래 시제는 미래에 대한 예상, 기대 등을 나타냅니다. 조동사 will과 be going to가 쓰이며, 조건절이나 시간의 부사절, 왕래발착 동사(come, go, arrive, leave, begin 등)의 경우에는 현재 시제가 미래의 의미를 나타내기도 합니다.

e.g. I **will do** my homework tomorrow. 나는 숙제를 내일 할 거야.

Judy **will be** here before her parents **pick** her up. Judy는 그녀의 부모님이 데리러 오기 전까지 여기 있을 것이다.

Everyone **is going to take** the test next Monday. 모두 다음 주 월요일에 시험을 볼 것이다.

The bus **arrives** at 7:00 this evening. 버스는 오늘 저녁 7시에 도착한다.

A 괄호 안에서 알맞은 것으로 고르시오.

01 Diane (washes, wash) her hair every other day.

02 My father (goes, went) to university twenty years ago.

03 I heard that light (travels, traveled) faster than sound.

04 The train for Seoul (left, leaves) in 10 minutes.

05 Some of his friends (visited, are going to visit) him last weekend.

06 The concert (begins, will begin) at 8:30 on Sundays.

07 The train (is going to leave, left) the station five minutes ago.

08 In the morning, the sun in my window (wakes, wake) me up.

09 I couldn't find the book, so I (went, will go) to the bookstore again tomorrow.

10 We will throw a party for John when he (goes, went) away.

B 문장에서 어법상 어색한 곳에 밑줄을 긋고 바르게 고치시오. 맞으면 O로 표시하시오.

01 I always eat breakfast in the morning. → ___________

02 Jack returns the book yesterday. → ___________

03 Alice will be in the classroom when the window broke. → ___________

04 The airplane departs in thirty minutes. → ___________

05 I lose my dictionary at the library last Friday. → ___________

06 The clothes dry well under the sun. → ___________

07 She usually laughed a lot when she watches TV. → ___________

08 The song I listened to yesterday was not good at all. → ___________

09 We will finish making dinner before you come tonight. → ___________

10 Water flowed from higher places to lower ones. → ___________

Check up 2

A 다음 계획표를 보고 문장을 완성하시오.

The First Week of Summer Vacation

	Monday	Tuesday	Wednesday	**Thursday** (TODAY)	Friday	Saturday/Sunday
I	buy some books	meet friends	go shopping	**go swimming**	write an essay	stay at home
Carrie	go swimming	go swimming	study English with friends	**go to see a movie**	go swimming	go camping

01 I ________________________ last Monday.

02 Carrie ________________________ with her friends yesterday.

03 I ________________________ yesterday.

04 I __________ some of my friends at the mall on Tuesday.

05 Carrie usually __________ swimming on weekdays.

06 I ________________________ an essay tomorrow.

07 I ________________________ at home this weekend.

08 Carrie ________________________ camping this weekend.

B 주어진 동사를 알맞은 시제로 바꾸어 대화를 완성하시오.

Anchor: Good morning. How is today's weather?

Forecaster: Please look outside the window. Can you believe it 01 ________ (rain) yesterday? Now you will see that it 02 ________ (be) very sunny. But in the afternoon, it 03 ________ (rain) a lot again. There 04 ________ (be) usually little rain this season. The weather 05 ________ (seem) strange these days, as many people think.

Anchor: I see. How's the weather of other countries around the world?

Forecaster: Well, it 06 ________ (snow) a lot yesterday in Australia, and it 07 ________ (snow) again tomorrow, too. And many people on the beaches in East Asia 08 ________ (escape) some powerful storms last night.

Actual Test

1 다음 빈칸에 들어가기에 알맞은 것은?

> Jamie usually _____ her hair in the morning.

① brush ② brushed ③ brushes
④ brushing ⑤ will brush

2 다음 중 어법상 어색한 문장은?

① I don't waste my time on shopping.
② Jane heard surprising news yesterday.
③ Everything will be changed next year.
④ I pick up these shells last weekend.
⑤ Bees make delicious honey.

3 다음 중 문장의 시제가 나머지와 다른 하나는?

① Water boils at 100 ℃.
② Jack kept a big secret from me.
③ The desert isn't a good place to live.
④ I take a piano lesson once a week.
⑤ Many countries send researchers to the Arctic.

4 다음 빈칸에 들어갈 말이 알맞게 짝지어진 것은?

> - This giraffe _(A)_ up to 4 meters later.
> - She _(B)_ beautiful photos at the zoo yesterday.
> - Whales live in the sea, but they _(C)_ air.

① will grow – took – breathed
② grows – will take – will breathe
③ grew – took – breathed
④ grew – took – breathe
⑤ will grow – took – breathe

[5-6] 다음 밑줄 친 부분 중 어법상 어색한 것은?

5 I hate horror movies, but I watch one with
①   ②   ③   ④
my friends last Saturday.
⑤

6 The space age began in the 1950's, and
①   ②
satellites continued to go into the space in
③   ④   ⑤
the future.

7 다음 질문에 가장 적절한 대답은?

> What is your plan for this weekend?

① I didn't do anything special.
② I'm going to clean my room.
③ I wanted to visit the History Museum.
④ I spend much time with my family.
⑤ I am very busy these days.

[8-9] 다음 문장을 주어진 시제로 바꾸어 쓰시오.

8 Jack didn't write a report for homework.
(현재)

→ _______________________________________

9 The scientists do research about weather.
(과거)

→ _______________________________________

10 주어진 단어들을 배열하여 글을 완성하시오.

> Miranda and I had a busy day. First, we went to the book store to buy some comic books. Then, _______________________________
> _______________________. (in the grocery store / some healthy snacks / we / bought)

I **have** already **eaten** lunch.

I **had been** at home for an hour
  when my mother arrived.

I **will have done** my work
  by next Sunday.

04 완료시제

현재완료

현재완료는 과거 특정 시점에 시작되어 현재에도 계속 영향을 끼치는 상황이나 행동을 나타내며, 「have + p.p.」
로 나타냅니다.

용법	예문	함께 쓰이는 부사
완료	I **have** already **eaten** lunch.	already, just, yet
경험	My sister **has been** to New York.	before, ever, often, once
결과	I **have lost** my wallet before.	before, ever, often, once
계속	Lisa **has known** Tom for a year.	for, since

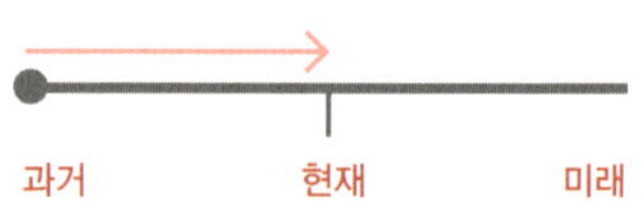

cf.) 현재완료는 과거의 특정 시점을 나타내는 부사구(yesterday, last night 등)와는 함께 쓰일 수 없습니다.

과거완료

과거완료는 과거의 특정 시점 이전의 상황이나 행동을 나타내며, 「had + p.p.」로 나타냅니다.

 I felt better after I **had taken** medicine.
나는 약을 먹고 난 후에 괜찮아졌다.
He **had finished** dinner when I got home.
그는 내가 집에 왔을 때 저녁을 다 먹은 상태였다.

미래완료

미래완료는 미래의 특정한 시점까지 완료되어 있을 일을 나타낼 때 쓰며,
「will have + p.p.」로 나타냅니다. 주로 「by + 시간(미래)」이나 「특정
기간 + from now」와 같이 미래 시간을 나타내는 어구와 함께 쓰입니다.

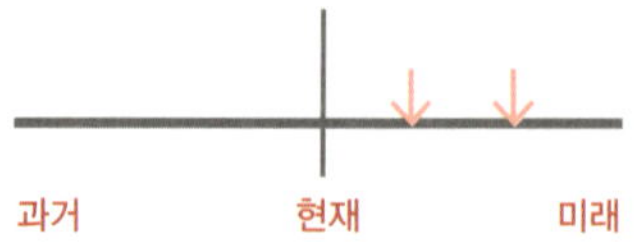

e.g. He **will have finished** the report by the time I arrive. 그는 내가 도착할 때까지 그 보고서를 끝낼 것이다.
My colleague **will have been** married a year from now. 내 직장 동료는 일년 후에는 결혼을 했을 것이다.

A 밑줄 친 동사를 알맞은 형태로 고치시오.

01 I have never <u>saw</u> a shooting star in the sky. → ____________

02 James told me that he <u>have</u> had a car accident. → ____________

03 Have you <u>draw</u> a picture of yourself? → ____________

04 I guess the man <u>have</u> never played the violin. → ____________

05 He <u>had</u> lived in Bagdad for five years next year. → ____________

06 My mom has never <u>sleeps</u> in a tent. → ____________

07 Have you ever <u>ride</u> a horse before? → ____________

08 I was sure that Lisa <u>has</u> cheated on the test before. → ____________

09 They <u>will have</u> lived in this house since 2001. → ____________

10 She <u>has</u> been working here for 3 years by next week. → ____________

B 주어진 말과 완료시제를 사용해 문장을 완성하시오.

01 I ________________ a lobster so far. (never, eat)

02 Tina ________________ Sarah for almost ten years. (know)

03 He ________________ any pictures since he lost his old camera. (not, take)

04 The concert ________________ by the time he gets here. (will, start)

05 Sam ________________ a businessman before he became a cook. (be)

06 The girl ________________ snow before. (never, see)

07 The zoo ________________ when I arrived there. (already, close)

08 When I got to the class, the teacher ________________ a quiz. (just, give)

09 She ________________ much free time since last semester. (not, have)

10 Do you know anyone who ________________ a lottery? (win)

Check up 2

A 다음 일과표를 보고 빈칸에 알맞은 말을 쓰시오.

	6 a.m.	9 a.m.	12 p.m.	3 p.m. NOW	6 p.m.	9 p.m.
I	(do nothing)	write a book review	have lunch at Jenny's		have dinner at home	post an essay on the website
Ann	go jogging	(do nothing)	Cook burgers at home	See a dentist	meet Sam at city Park	chat online with friends

01 I _____________________ a book review before I had lunch at Jenny's.

02 Ann _____________________ before I wrote a book review.

03 I _____________________ nothing until 9 a.m.

04 Ann _____________________ burgers before she left home to see a dentist.

05 Now, I _____________________ at Jenny's with my friends.

06 Ann __________ just __________ a dentist.

07 Ann _____________________ am at City Park by the time I have dinner at home.

08 I _____________________ my essay online by 10 p.m. tonight.

B 주어진 말과 완료시제를 사용해 대화를 완성하시오.

> *Jack*: Do you like traveling?
>
> *Bora*: Yes. I do like traveling.
>
> *Jack*: What countries **01** _____________________ (visit, you) so far?
>
> *Bora*: Hmm, I **02** _____________________ (be) to the U.S., Japan, and China.
>
> *Jack*: I **03** _____________________ (be, never) to any of those countries. But I **04** _____________________ (travel) to Russia. I **05** _____________________ (go) to Moscow when I was there.
>
> *Bora*: That's interesting! I **06** _____________________ (want, always) to go there.
>
> *Jack*: But I **07** _____________________ (have) many chances to travel abroad. Do you have any plans to go abroad this year?
>
> *Bora*: Yes! I **08** _____________________ (leave) this country when summer break starts!

Actual Test

[1-2] 다음 빈칸에 들어가기에 알맞은 것은?

1

> I have ________ math to my younger sister.

① teach   ② teaching   ③ taught
④ been taught ⑤ been teached

2

> He ________ with his parents until yesterday.

① never fights   ② is never fighting
③ has never fought   ④ had never fought
⑤ will have never fought

3 다음 중 빈칸에 들어갈 알맞은 말끼리 짝지어진 것은?

> - How many times ___(A)___ he slept during class so far?
> - Sam ___(B)___ finished reading when he called me.

① has – had   ② had – had
③ have – had   ④ had – has
⑤ has – has

4 다음 중 어법상 어색한 문장은?

① I haven't had dinner yet.
② There had been no one here before I came in.
③ It has snowed a lot until now.
④ We've been to the store before.
⑤ He has finished the report by the time I arrive.

5 다음 중 빈칸에 들어갈 수 <u>없는</u> 것은?

> I haven't watched the movie ________.

① yet   ② yesterday   ③ so far
④ until now   ⑤ before

[6-7] 다음 밑줄 친 부분 중 어법상 <u>어색한</u> 것은?

6 I didn't think that they had lost the game.
       ①   ②   ③
The referee haven't made a fair call.
             ④   ⑤

7 Tom has to clean the house before his
                  ①
wife has arrived. So far, he has cleaned just
     ②   ③   ④   ⑤
the kitchen.

[8-9] 다음 문장을 주어진 지시에 따라 바꾸어 쓰시오.

8 He has found his wallet. (부정문)

→ ________________________________

9 You have enjoyed yourself at the party. (의문문)

→ ________________________________

10 주어진 단어들을 배열하여 글을 완성하시오.

> John has read three novels since the beginning of this semester. He ________
> ________________, (before / read / many novels / has) but this is the first time he has read English novels.

When I got home, my little brother **was riding** a bike.

He **had been riding** it for two hours.

05 진행형

단순 진행형

진행형은 말을 하는 시점에 어떤 일이 진행 중이거나 지속되는 상황을 나타내며, 「be + -ing」의 형태로 씁니다.

	단순시제	진행형
현재	Tom **watches** TV *every day*. (평소의 반복적 행동)	Tom **is watching** TV *right now*. (현재의 상황)
과거	I **ate** a lot of Italian food *yesterday*. (과거 시점에 일어난 일)	I **was eating** a lot of Italian food *when my mom called me*. (과거의 특정 시점에 진행되고 있던 일)
미래	They **will visit** China *next week*. (미래에 일어날 일)	They **will be visiting** China *this time next week*. (미래의 특정 시점에 진행되고 있을 상황)

 I **was walking** down the street *at 10 a.m. yesterday*. 나는 어제 오전 10시에 길을 걷고 있었다.
We **won't be working** *this time next week*. 우린 다음 주 이 시간에는 사무실에서 일하고 있지 않을 것이다.

완료 진행형

완료 진행형은 이전에 시작된 행동이나 상황이 말을 하는 시점까지 계속되고 있는 경우에 쓰며, 동작이 지속되어 왔다는 사실을 강조합니다. 「have been + -ing」의 형태로 나타냅니다.

	완료 진행형
현재	I **have been having** dinner *for two hours*. (현재까지 지속되고 있는 행동)
과거	Eric **had been reading** for an hour *when she came*. (이전부터 과거의 특정 시점까지 지속되고 있던 일)
미래	He **will have been hiking** the mountain for three days *when he gets to the top*. (미래의 특정 시점까지 진행되고 있을 일)

We **had been talking** before the café closed. 우리는 카페가 닫기 전까지 계속 얘기하고 있었다.
He **will have been sleeping** until we come back. 그는 우리가 돌아올 때까지 계속 자고 있을 것이다.

A 밑줄 친 부분을 진행시제로 바꾸어 쓰시오.

01 She is make a kite for her children now. → __________

02 The little robot was clean the room when I came in. → __________

03 Gary will being taking his English class at this time tomorrow. → __________

04 I have been painted the old furniture for my mom. → __________

05 The rain had be falling for almost a day. → __________

06 The boy was being played the guitar when I entered the hall. → __________

07 My little brother is pours water for everyone right now. → __________

08 We will been having waiting for an hour by the time it opens. → __________

09 People had having using robots for hard work before the 1990s. → __________

10 The plane has being flying over the Pacific Ocean for an hour. → __________

B 괄호 안에서 알맞은 것을 고르시오.

01 The rocket (rises, is rising) in the sky right now.

02 You (weren't reading, didn't read) a book when I came in.

03 There (was, was being) a car accident here last night.

04 Jack (has been writing, writes) his final essay since noon.

05 She (will have been sleeping, have been sleeping) for ten hours when I get home.

06 I (am riding, will be riding) a bike in Jeju island this time next weekend.

07 He (talks, has been talking) to his girlfriend for an hour now.

08 Julia always (goes, has been gone) to bed before midnight.

09 I (had been swimming, swim) at this gym when you called me.

10 Aunt Mary (watches, has been watching) the documentary all morning.

A 다음 그림을 보고 주어진 동사를 사용해 문장을 완성하시오.

| Two hours ago | Now |

01 The old man ______________ (read) the newspaper when I saw him.

02 The old man ______________ (read) the newspaper for two hours.

03 The woman with long hair ______________ (draw) a picture when the man came up with his dog.

04 The man with a dog ______________ (take) a walk two hours ago.

05 The man on the bicycle ______________ (ride) it very slowly now.

06 The man and woman ______________ (play) badminton now.

07 I guess the man and woman ______________ (play) badminton for two hours.

B 다음 글에서 밑줄 친 부분을 바르게 고치시오.

John and I usually **01** <u>doesn't enjoy</u> traveling, but we **02** <u>had deciding</u> to give it a try. We **03** <u>has been planning</u> to go to New York. John **04** <u>had been watched</u> a movie on TV, and then there **05** <u>is</u> a beautiful scene in Italy. Since then, we **06** <u>had been searching</u> for the information about the country until now. Right now, we **07** <u>look</u> for a hotel to stay in. We're so excited. We **08** <u>have been walking</u> on the streets of Rome at this time next month!

01 ________________   **02** ________________   **03** ________________

04 ________________   **05** ________________   **06** ________________

07 ________________   **08** ________________

Actual Test

1 다음 빈칸에 들어가기에 알맞은 것은?

> I __________ to school this time tomorrow.

① walked　　② walk　　③ am walking
④ was walking　⑤ will be walking

2 밑줄 친 부분이 어법상 어색한 것은?

① Did she <u>bake</u> a cake yesterday?
② You <u>are paying not</u> attention right now.
③ The eagle <u>was flying</u> high in the sky.
④ The man <u>is complaining</u> about the weather.
⑤ Will you <u>be playing</u> the piano later?

3 다음 중 어법상 어색한 문장은?

① Will you be standing here when I come back?
② Is your mom doing laundry now?
③ The boys were catching butterflies yesterday.
④ He has been working when I came back to the office.
⑤ She has been talking to her friends for hours.

4 다음 답에 대한 질문으로 적절한 것은?

> No, he hasn't.

① Was he doing exercises at that time?
② Is he doing exercises right now?
③ Will he be doing exercises in two hours?
④ Has he been doing exercises so far?
⑤ Had he been doing exercises until then?

5 다음 빈칸에 들어갈 말이 알맞게 짝지어진 것은?

> I __(A)__ calls to my friends since I __(B)__ home.

① am making – am coming
② have been making – am coming
③ had been making – coming
④ had been making – come
⑤ have been making – came

[6-7] 다음 밑줄 친 부분 중 어법상 어색한 것은?

6 I <u>had been waiting</u>① for <u>my cousin</u>② <u>at the</u>③ <u>airport</u>④ for an hour <u>so far</u>⑤.

7 A thief <u>broke</u>① <u>into</u>② the house <u>while</u>③ the boys <u>are watching</u>④ TV <u>last</u>⑤ night.

[8-9] 주어진 단어들을 배열하여 다음 전화 대화를 완성하시오. 필요한 경우 형태를 바꾸시오.

> **A:** How **8** (have / be / you / do)?
> **B:** Good! I've been having dinner at home. Why **9** (call / me / you / do)?
> **A:** I wanted to ask you something.

8 __________　　**9** __________

10 다음 밑줄 친 부분을 바르게 고치시오.

> I've been practicing soccer before an important match. The match is next week. <u>I am running the ground</u> to win the game this time next Tuesday!

→ __________

Review Test

[1-4] 다음 빈칸에 들어가기에 알맞은 것은?

01

Jane _______ her horse every morning.

① feed   ② feeds   ③ feeding
④ feeded   ⑤ to feed

02

I _______ my guests Italian food yesterday.

① serve   ② serves   ③ serving
④ served   ⑤ am serving

03

He _______ his trip to Jeju island right now.

① plan   ② planning   ③ was planning
④ planned   ⑤ is planning

04

The dog _______ all day.

① has been eating   ② will be sleeping
③ was barking   ④ caught birds
⑤ is going out

[5-6] 다음 중 빈칸에 들어갈 수 <u>없는</u> 것은?

05

Bill _______ last night.

① was sleeping   ② took a test
③ reads a book   ④ didn't watch TV
⑤ was chatting online

06

I _______ tomorrow morning.

① will jog   ② am going to watch TV
③ will do yoga   ④ will take a walk
⑤ will have written the letter

[7-9] 다음 중 어법상 <u>틀린</u> 문장을 고르시오.

07

① Children has asked for new snow sleds.
② Many birds have traveled south already.
③ I am looking forward to my aunt's visit.
④ Has your father fixed his car yet?
⑤ My sister is living in an apartment.

08

① The men are checking their trucks.
② I was setting up a tent for camping.
③ Jack had been playing computer games.
④ The train departed on time an hour ago.
⑤ The weather has being bad for weeks.

09

① He hasn't found his wallet yet.
② I was drinking water at the park.
③ You will had seen famous pictures in the museum.
④ Water rises into the air and becomes clouds.
⑤ The leaves had already changed their color.

[10-12] 다음 중 어법에 맞는 문장을 고르시오.

10

① We had won the game tomorrow.

② A strong wind is blowing yesterday.

③ Last night, Tim will be brushing his teeth.

④ He worked overnight right now.

⑤ We'll have completed the project by next week.

11

① I was enjoying my vacation right now.

② A mother hasn't fed her child tomorrow.

③ We were riding a train when you were at home.

④ She takes a walk when it was sunny.

⑤ Dorothy didn't remember her dream tomorrow.

12

① She is taking pictures when I saw her.

② The plane will be leaving an hour ago.

③ The lion had been watching you now.

④ He has given me presents next week.

⑤ Birds fly south for the winter every year.

[13-14] 빈칸에 들어갈 말이 알맞게 짝지어진 것을 고르시오.

13

> • We ___(A)___ looked everywhere for the missing pen until now.
>
> • We ___(B)___ waiting for the rally to begin now.

① are – had
② were – have
③ have – are
④ had – were
⑤ were – are

14

> **A:** ___(A)___ you ever been to Japan?
> **B:** No, I haven't, but I have ___(B)___ to China.

① Had – been
② Have – been
③ Have – was
④ Have – be
⑤ Had – being

[15-16] 빈칸에 공통으로 들어가기에 알맞은 것을 고르시오.

15

> • The singer ______ just memorized all the lyrics.
>
> • Joel ______ two sisters and one brother.

① were
② was
③ have
④ has
⑤ been

16

> • The fisherman ______ working overnight this evening.
>
> • Jay ______ taking drum lessons when he becomes a university student.

① was being
② was
③ will be
④ is
⑤ is being

[17-19] 주어진 단어들을 바르게 배열하시오.

17 (the lawn / Anthony / cut / had)

→ _________________________ before I came home.

18 (in the choir / the twins / sung / for three years / have)

→ _________________________

_________________________ now.

19 (eating / will / you / been / have)

→ _________________________

when Mr. Lee comes back?

[20-21] 다음 우리말을 영어로 알맞게 옮긴 것을 고르시오.

20

Sue는 아름다운 무지개를 보고 있었다.

① Sue looks at the beautiful rainbow.
② Sue is looking at the beautiful rainbow.
③ Sue had looked at the beautiful rainbow.
④ Sue looked at the beautiful rainbow.
⑤ Sue was looking at the beautiful rainbow.

21

그는 몇 시간째 말하고 있었던 중이었다.

① He talked for hours.
② He is talking for hours.
③ He has been talking for hours.
④ He had been talking for hours.
⑤ He will have been talking for hours.

[22-23] 어법상 어색한 부분을 찾아 바르게 고치시오.

22 _________ → _________

Many people had wished for a mild winter. But there is a big snow storm last month.

23 _________ → _________

It snowed heavily yesterday. Some students have missing school today because of the snow.

[24-25] 다음 글을 읽고 물음에 답하시오.

People ① love ice cream. Funny thing is that no one ② knows for sure who invented it. At first, Roman emperor Nero ③ served sweet snow for dessert. Later, in the 1660s, wealthy Europeans ④ enjoyed a rare treat – "water ice." Cooks added cream to the ice. Unlike today, making ice cream ⑤ takes hours then. But some things about ice cream ___(A)___ (change) even now. People try various flavors as they did in the past!

24 밑줄 친 부분 중 어법상 어색한 것은?

①　　　②　　　③　　　④　　　⑤

25 주어진 동사를 알맞은 형태로 바꾸어 빈칸 (A)를 채우시오.

→ _________________________

조동사

A : Rich people **can spend** much money.

B : I think they **shouldn't do** that.
They **ought to give** some money
to poor people.

조동사 1 (능력/허가/추측/의무)

능력·허가: can(could), may

조동사 can(could)은 '~할 수 있다'는 의미로 능력을 나타내며, be able to와 바꾸어 쓸 수 있습니다. '~해도 된다'는 허가의 의미를 나타내는 조동사에는 can과 may가 있습니다.

능력	can	I **can speak(=am able to speak)** a foreign language. 나는 외국어를 한 가지 말할 수 있다.
		My father **could lift(=was able to lift)** me high. (과거형) 우리 아버지는 나를 위로 높이 들어올릴 수 있으셨다.
허가	can	If you don't finish your meal, you **cannot have** dessert. 밥을 다 먹지 않으면 넌 디저트를 먹을 수 없어.
	may	A: **May I go** outside to hang out with my friends? 밖에 나가서 친구들이랑 놀아도 되나요? B: No, you **may not**. Just stay home. 아니, 안돼. 그냥 집에 있으렴.

추측: may, might, could, must

may, might, could는 '~일 수 있다'는 의미이며, must는 '~임에 틀림없다'는 강한 추측을 나타냅니다.

e.g. He **may be** very sick. 그는 매우 아픈 걸지도 몰라.
The man **might send** flowers to Jenny. 그 남자가 Jenny에게 꽃을 보냈을 것이다.
The thief **could be** out of our town now. 그 도둑은 지금 우리 마을을 벗어났을 거예요.
You **must have** the wrong number. There is no one by that name here.
전화를 잘못 거신 게 틀림없네요. 그런 이름을 가진 사람은 없어요.

c.f. cannot은 '~일리 없다'는 강한 불가능성을 나타냅니다.　It **cannot be** true. 그것은 사실일 리가 없어.

의무·조언: must, should, ought to, had better

must는 '~해야만 한다'는 의미로, have to와 바꾸어 쓸 수 있습니다. should는 must보다는 약한 의무를 나타내며, ought to와 had better는 조언을 할 때 씁니다.

e.g. You **must(= have to) tell** me the truth in court. 법정에서는 진실만을 말해야 합니다.
You **should(= ought to, had better) stop** talking. 네가 이야기를 그만해야 해.

A 밑줄 친 단어와 바꾸어 쓸 수 있는 것을 고르시오.

01 <u>May</u> I use your cell phone for a minute?　(Must, Can)

02 You <u>must</u> put on sunscreen cream in the summer.　(could, should)

03 I think the man <u>might</u> come from India.　(should, may)

04 You <u>cannot</u> enter this building without an ID card.　(may not, must not)

05 My father <u>ought to</u> know that I did my best.　(could, should)

06 I told my father that he <u>had better</u> quit smoking.　(ought to, may)

07 The fact that we lost the game <u>must not</u> be true.　(should not, cannot)

08 If you want to travel abroad, you <u>should</u> have a passport.

　(must, could)

09 You <u>may</u> send text messages after class.　(can, could)

10 The movie <u>may</u> be difficult for children.　(must, might)

B 밑줄 친 부분을 바르게 고치시오.

01 Do I <u>must</u> bring my own food for the party?　→ ___________

02 The man <u>could</u> able to take the train in time.　→ ___________

03 He <u>might left</u> our soccer team because of his illness.　→ ___________

04 You'd <u>not better</u> call him tomorrow.　→ ___________

05 The rumor that he stole the bag <u>can be not</u> true.　→ ___________

06 <u>Can</u> you able to solve this math problem?　→ ___________

07 I guess he <u>must have to see</u> a doctor right now.　→ ___________

08 He <u>might to have</u> lots of friends because he's very kind.　→ ___________

09 You should <u>throw not</u> away the garbage.　→ ___________

10 <u>May I be able to cross</u> the road now?　→ ___________

Check up 2

A 다음 가족들의 습관을 참고하여 보기에서 알맞은 말을 골라 문장을 완성하시오.

I	bite my fingernails	Grandmother	talk too much
Father	smoke too much	Sister	drink too much coffee
Mother	play with her hair	Brother	keep scratching all the time

had better tie	may like	should not bite
might be awake	might need	ought to quit

01 I _________________ my fingernails because it sometimes hurts.

02 My grandmother talks too much. She _______________ to talk very much.

03 My father _________________ smoking for his health.

04 My mother _________________ her hair when cooking. I sometimes see her hair in food.

05 My sister drinks too much coffee, so I guess she _________________ late at night.

06 My brother _________________ to see a doctor because he scratches himself too much.

B 괄호 안의 말을 바르게 써서 대화를 완성하시오.

Son: Mom, **01** _________________ (may, take a rest, I) at home today?

Mom: Well, I think you **02** _________________ (can, to school, go) today. You don't have a fever.

Son: But I **03** _________________ (might, sick, get) later today. I **04** _____________ (kept, be, should) in good condition because I **05** _________________ (must, football, play) tomorrow. No one else can take my place.

Mom: Hmm, okay. I **06** _________________ (can, stay, you, let) home today. But **07** _________________ (had better, ask, you) your friends what they learned today.

Actual Test

1 다음 밑줄 친 단어와 바꾸어 쓸 수 있는 것은?

> The report <u>may</u> not be true.

① can　　② should　　③ must
④ might　　⑤ ought to

2 다음 빈칸에 들어가기에 알맞은 것은?

> The soccer player _______ be careful of injury while playing the game.

① can　　② may　　③ might
④ could　　⑤ should

3 다음 중 어법상 <u>어색한</u> 문장은?

① Can I speak to the manager here?
② You don't have to be sorry for me.
③ Jack cannot be able to speak Korean.
④ The man ought to know the truth.
⑤ You must bring food to my party.

4 다음 문장의 밑줄 친 부분과 쓰임이 같은 것은?

> The man <u>might</u> live near my apartment.

① You <u>can</u> use the Internet in our café.
② Cats <u>can</u> jump from high places.
③ The fat clown <u>could</u> be my uncle.
④ You <u>should</u> wash your hands often.
⑤ You <u>had better</u> leave now, or you'll miss the plane.

[5-6] 다음 밑줄 친 부분 중 어법상 <u>어색한</u> 것은?

5 A: <u>Do</u> we <u>have to</u> <u>wake up</u> early
　　　①　　②　　③
　　tomorrow?

B: No, you <u>don't have to</u>. But you <u>must have to</u>
　　　　　④　　　　　　　　　⑤
leave the hotel before 11 am.

6 Many singers <u>can sing</u> their songs very
　　　　　　　　①
well. But I think Jerry is <u>the only one</u> <u>who</u>
　　　　　　　　②　　　　　　　③
<u>is able to</u> <u>can touch</u> people's hearts with his
　　④　　　　⑤
songs.

7 다음 중 의미가 나머지와 <u>다른</u> 하나는?

① He may be out of town by now.
② He might be out of town by now.
③ He could be out of town by now.
④ He can be out of town by now.
⑤ He ought to be out of town by now.

[8-9] 두 문장의 뜻이 일치하도록 주어진 말을 사용해 영작하시오.

8 We should prepare for global warming. (had better)

= ________________________________

9 A helicopter can stay at one point. (be able to)

= ________________________________

10 다음 주어진 대답에 적절한 질문을 완성하시오.

> Q: ________________________________
> A: Yes, you may leave early today.

A: **Will** you carry all these boxes?

B: I have to, but I need help.

   Would you please give me a hand?

조동사 2 (미래 / 의지 / 과거 습관 / 부탁)

미래·의지: will

조동사 will은 '~할 것이다'는 뜻으로, 미래에 일어날 일이나 주어의 의지를 표현할 때 씁니다.

e.g. He **will not come,** whatever you say. 네가 뭐라고 하든 그는 오지 않을 거야.

I told him that I **would hang** out tonight. (과거형) 나는 오늘 밤 놀 거라고 그에게 말했다.

David **will buy** (= **is going to buy**) a pet next month. David는 다음 달에 애완동물 한 마리를 살 계획이다.

과거 습관: used to, would

used to는 과거의 규칙적인 습관을 나타내며, '~하곤 했었다. (하지만 지금은 그렇지 않다.)'라는 뜻입니다.
would는 과거의 불규칙적인 습관 및 상태를 나타냅니다.

e.g. He **used to live** in California. (현재에는 해당하지 않는 경우) 그는 캘리포니아에 살았었다.

My father **would read** me a story when I was a kid. (불규칙적)
내가 아이였을 때. 아버지는 나에게 이야기를 읽어주곤 했었다.

공손한 부탁: will, would, can, could

공손하게 부탁을 할 경우에는 조동사 will, would, can, could로 시작하는 의문문을 쓰며, '~해도 될까요?'
라는 의미를 나타냅니다.

e.g. **Will** you (please) **close** the door for us? 우릴 위해 그 문 좀 닫아줄 수 있을까요?

Would you **lend** me your phone for a minute? 당신의 전화기를 잠시만 빌려주시겠어요?

Can you **give** us a break? 저희에게 휴식 시간을 좀 주실 수 있나요?

Could you **keep** an eye on my bag here? 여기 있는 제 가방 좀 봐주시겠습니까?

A　괄호 안에서 알맞은 것을 고르시오.

01 Jed (will study, will studying) either law or business in college.

02 I'm sure that John (will not be, will be not) here tomorrow evening.

03 Our family (is going to go, is going to going) camping this summer.

04 I think they (will going to, are going to) take the next train.

05 He (could came, could come) home very late at that time.

06 My aunt (would visit, would visiting) us on our birthdays.

07 Ms. Smith (used to give, used to giving) extra lessons to students after school.

08 (Would, Are) you pass me the sugar on the table?

09 Could you (giving, give) me some time to think before the decision?

10 Our school (used sending, used to send) many students to good universities.

B　주어진 말을 사용하여 문장을 완성하시오. be동사의 경우 알맞은 형태로 쓰시오.

01 My relatives from the U.S. _________________ me next week. (be going to, visit)

02 Joe _________________ on the math test. (would, well, do)

03 I _________________ with my brother on weekends. (used to, to, concerts, go)

04 _________________ my secret for me? (keep, you, can)

05 Too much fat _________________ you gain weight. (be going to, make)

06 _________________ in China 3 years ago. (live, the family, used to)

07 _________________ dinner here tonight? (be going to, have, we)

08 The tree _________________ very small when I was young. (be, used to)

09 _________________ the cereal and milk before you come home? (buy, you, could, me)

Check up 2

A 다음 도시 계획표를 보고 밑줄 친 부분을 would/used to 또는 will/be going to를 써서 바르게 고치시오.

City Plan

	Population	Market	A landmark building
Past	50,000	local markets and small stores	a ball park and small ice rink
Present	100,000	supermarkets	a stadium under construction
Future	500,000	a big market and a multiplex	three big stadiums for Olympic games

01 There <u>will be</u> fifty thousand people in the past. → __________

02 The city <u>would have</u> 500,000 people in the future. → __________

03 More people <u>used to come</u> to the city in the future. → __________

04 The city <u>was going to build</u> a multiplex next year. → __________

05 People <u>were going to buy</u> things at small local markets. → __________

06 People <u>will enjoy</u> skating in the city's ice rink. → __________

07 There <u>was going to be</u> a ball park in the city. → __________

08 The city <u>could have</u> Olympic stadiums. → __________

B 주어진 말을 사용해 글을 완성하시오. be동사의 경우 알맞은 형태로 쓰시오.

Dear Manager of Cinephil Theater:

I **01** __________________ (go, to your theater, used to) often, but when I went to a movie last Saturday, I almost fell over. The floor was too sticky! The theater **02** __________________ (very clean, be, used to). But these days, it's dirty and dangerous. The restroom was also dirty. I said to a manager, "**03** __________________ (clean, the restroom, you, would) now, please?" But he just ignored me. Your theater **04** __________________ (me, impress, used to) in the past, but it doesn't anymore. If **05** __________________ (solve, be going to, you, not) this problem, **06** __________________ (will, complain, I) to the government office myself.

Actual Test

1 다음 밑줄 친 부분이 어법상 어색한 것은?

① The cat <u>would hide</u> when someone came.
② Jack <u>was used to be</u> afraid of flying.
③ <u>Could you let</u> me make a call?
④ I <u>used to be</u> a very shy boy.
⑤ <u>Would you give</u> me a big hug and kiss?

2 다음 밑줄 친 부분의 쓰임이 다른 하나는?

① I <u>would</u> play the game a lot a year ago.
② You <u>would</u> go out with Jack before.
③ It <u>would</u> rain hard in summer back then.
④ <u>Would</u> you give me more time?
⑤ He <u>would</u> take care of me when I was a child.

3 다음 밑줄 친 단어와 바꾸어 쓸 수 있는 것은?

Sam <u>would</u> lead the parade before.

① could　　② should　　③ had to
④ used to　　⑤ was going to

4 다음 우리말을 영어로 알맞게 옮긴 것은?

나는 친구들이 내 자전거를 못 타게 하곤 했다.

① I could never let my friends ride my bike.
② I would not let my friends ride my bike.
③ I was not going to let my friends ride my bike.
④ I used to not let my friends ride my bike.
⑤ I wasn't used to let my friends ride my bike.

5 When my grandma had a cold, her mother would made her hot lemon tea.
(밑줄 ①~⑤)

6 When I was a child, I used take a book to the restroom because I liked reading.
(밑줄 ①~⑤)

[5-6] 다음 밑줄 친 부분 중 어법상 어색한 것은?

5 <u>When</u> my grandma <u>had</u> a cold, <u>her</u> mother
　　　①　　　　　　　②　　　　　③
<u>would made</u> her <u>hot</u> lemon tea.
　　④　　　　　⑤

6 When I <u>was</u> <u>a child</u>, I <u>used take</u> a book
　　　　①　　②　　　　　③
to the restroom because I <u>liked</u> <u>reading</u>.
　　　　　　　　　　　　④　　　⑤

7 다음 대화의 우리말을 영어로 알맞게 옮긴 것은?

A: 줄에서 기다려주시겠습니까?
B: Oh, I'm sorry. I didn't see the line.

① Do you please wait in line?
② Are you going to wait in line, please?
③ Are you used to wait in line, please?
④ You can't please wait in line?
⑤ Will you please wait in line?

[8-9] 주어진 단어들을 바르게 배열하시오.

8 (fat and unhealthy / used to / he / be)

→ _______________________________________

before he quit smoking.

9 (for me / can / the air conditioner / turn off / you)

→ _______________________________ ?

10 주어진 동사와 알맞은 조동사를 사용해 글을 완성하시오.

I remember Ms. Kim's first grade class.
Each morning, Ms. Kim (A)_____________
(sit) at her desk. She (B)_____________
(smile) and say hello to each student.

Sam got on the wrong bus.

He **should have checked** the bus number.

He **might have been** very busy.

08 조동사의 과거 (후회/추측)

유감·후회: should/could have + p.p.

조동사의 과거는 「조동사＋have＋과거분사(p.p.)」로 나타내며, 과거 일에 대한 후회와 유감을 나타냅니다.

e.g. You **should have talked** to your parents first. 너는 네 부모님과 먼저 말을 했어야 했어.
I **should have finished** the report first. 나는 그 보고서를 먼저 끝냈어야 했다.(보고서를 끝내지 못한 사실을 후회함)
You **shouldn't have listened** to him. 너는 그의 말을 듣지 말았어야 했어.(그의 말을 들었다는 사실을 후회함)

I **could have taken** the bus, but I took a taxi. 나는 버스를 탈 수도 있었지만, 택시를 탔다.
She **could have checked** my messages, but she didn't.
그녀는 내 메시지를 확인할 수도 있었지만, 그렇게 하지 않았다.
I **could have met** you today, but I didn't want to. 나는 오늘 널 만날 수도 있었지만, 그러고 싶지 않았어.

추측: must/cannot/may/might have + p.p.

조동사의 과거는 또한 과거 일에 대한 추측을 나타냅니다. 「must have＋p.p.」는 '~였음에 틀림없다'는
의미이며, 「cannot have＋p.p.」는 '~였을 리가 없다', 「may/might have＋p.p.」는 '~였을지도 모른다'
는 의미입니다.

e.g. Sally **must have cheated** on the math test yesterday. Sally는 어제 수학 시험에서 부정행위를 했음에 틀림없다.
He **must have gone** to school today. 그는 오늘 학교에 갔음에 틀림없다.

Sam **cannot have told** him my secret. Sam이 그에게 내 비밀을 말했을 리가 없어.
She **cannot have left** home without her cell phone. 그녀가 휴대폰 없이 집을 나갔을 리가 없다.

The **man might have made** several mistakes on the report. 그가 보고서에서 몇 가지 실수를 했을 수도 있다.
The dog **may have eaten** all the bread. 그 개가 빵을 전부 먹어버렸을지도 몰라.

I was not sure, but she **might have seen** the criminal.
확신할 수는 없었지만, 그녀는 범인을 보았을지도 모른다.

A 주어진 말을 사용하여 조동사의 과거형을 쓰시오.

01 You _________________ the police first. (should, call)

02 My father _________________ the car yesterday. (may, fix)

03 The cat _________________ in the closet. (might, hide)

04 The soccer player _________________ the ball with his hands. (must, touch)

05 I _________________ Ann to help me with my report. (could, ask)

06 We _________________ for the rain to stop. (should not, wait)

07 You _________________ me the truth, but you lied to me. (could, tell)

08 Sam _________________ this photo himself. (cannot, take)

B 다음 문장을 주어진 조동사를 사용하여 바꾸어 쓰시오.

01 I had a stomachache, but I didn't see a doctor. (should)

→ I _________________________ because I had a stomachache.

02 The train was not on time, so I couldn't arrive in Seoul early. (could)

→ If the train were on time, I _________________________.

03 I brought her a drink because I thought she was thirsty. (might)

→ I brought her a drink because she _________________________.

04 John was drunk, so I thought he didn't drive the car himself. (may)

→ Because he was drunk, John _________________________ himself.

05 She caught that flight, so she was in Busan. (may)

→ She _________________________ if she hadn't have caught that flight.

06 It was April, so I thought the snow on the mountain melted. (might)

→ The snow on the mountain _________________________ because it was April.

07 Jay was sleeping, so I was sure that he couldn't write the email. (cannot)

→ Jay _________________________ because he was sleeping.

08 The roads are frozen. I think it snowed hard last night. (must)

→ It _________________________ because the roads are frozen.

Check up 2

A 다음은 Peggy네 반 학생들이 과거에 하지 못해 아쉬운 일을 적은 표이다. 조동사 should나 could를 이용하여 문장을 완성하시오.

	Things I regret	Things I could do
Peggy	late for school today	choose where to go for the field trip
Jack	not listen to Paul's advice	buy the latest game CD for half price
Jane	prepare for the concert early	stand right in front of the singer
Paul	go to bed early last night	see the beautiful sunrise

01 Peggy _________________________ late for school today.

02 Peggy _________________________ where to go for the school field trip.

03 Jack _________________________ to Paul's advice.

04 Jack _________________________ the latest game CD for half price.

05 Jane _________________________ for the concert early this morning.

06 Jane _________________________ right in front of the singer on stage.

07 Paul _________________________ to bed early last night.

08 Paul _________________________ the beautiful sunrise on the beach.

B 다음 글에서 밑줄 친 부분을 바르게 고치시오.

It's lunch time in class. Paula fell asleep in her seat. She **01** <u>must stay up</u> late last night. George went out of the classroom to meet his friend. He **02** <u>may go</u> to meet John in the next class. Marie asked her teacher if she could go out for an hour. She **03** <u>might leave</u> her homework at home. Peter and Lisa are going to the cafeteria. They **04** <u>may forget</u> to bring their lunch this morning. Sam is eating lunch very fast. He **05** <u>must be</u> very hungry this morning.

01 _______________ **02** _______________ **03** _______________

04 _______________ **05** _______________

Actual Test

1 다음 밑줄 친 단어의 형태가 틀린 것은?

① The typhoon must have <u>leave</u> this city.
② You should have <u>hidden</u> your math score.
③ The train must have <u>departed</u> an hour ago.
④ She might not have <u>read</u> the newspaper.
⑤ Helen may have <u>called</u> him last night.

2 다음 빈칸에 들어가기에 알맞은 것은?

> You look so sick. You _______ to school today.

① should have came
② should have not come
③ should have not came
④ shouldn't have came
⑤ shouldn't have come

3 다음 우리말을 영어로 알맞게 옮긴 것은?

> 나는 캠핑을 갈 수도 있었다.

① I must have gone camping.
② I will have gone camping
③ I could have gone camping.
④ I should have gone camping.
⑤ I cannot have gone camping.

4 다음 빈칸에 들어갈 말이 알맞게 짝지어진 것은?

> • I should have ___(A)___ at the mall yesterday.
> • Sam cannot have ___(B)___ this magazine.

① be – brought
② be – bring
③ been – brought
④ been – bring
⑤ being – bringing

5 다음 문장에 이어질 내용으로 가장 적절한 것은?

> My brother lost his wallet at the football game.

① He must have left it at home.
② He shouldn't have been careful.
③ He couldn't have known where it was.
④ He could have known where he left it.
⑤ He should have been more careful.

[6-7] 다음 밑줄 친 부분 중 어법상 어색한 것은?

6 I <u>failed</u> the English test. I <u>might</u> have <u>write</u> many <u>wrong</u> words.
① ② ③ ④ ⑤

7 Your sweater <u>might</u> <u>be</u> the same one as <u>mine</u>. You <u>should</u> <u>have not bought</u> it.
① ② ③ ④ ⑤

[8-9] 주어진 단어들을 바르게 배열하시오.

8 (cannot / my call / ignored / he / have)

→ _______________________________

9 (the volume / the staff / turned down / have / could)

→ _______________________________

10 주어진 동사와 알맞은 조동사를 사용하여 글을 완성하시오.

> I gave 10 dollars to my brother yesterday. I thought he had some money to buy books, but he didn't have any. He _____________ (spend) it all in a single day.

Review Test

[1-3] 다음 빈칸에 들어가기에 알맞은 것은?

01 

> He might ________ good care of his bike.

① take   ② takes   ③ took
④ taking   ⑤ taken

02

> Could you please ________ aside for the
> wheelchair to go through?

① be stepped   ② steps   ③ stepped
④ step   ⑤ stepping

03

> You should have ________ to my advice.

① listen   ② listens   ③ listening
④ to listen   ⑤ listened

[4-6] 다음 빈칸에 들어갈 수 <u>없는</u> 것을 고르시오.

04 

> She ________ been in the office last Sunday.

① cannot have   ② must have
③ could not   ④ may have
⑤ might have

05

> ________ you carry those heavy boxes for me?

① Will   ② Can   ③ Would
④ Could   ⑤ Have

06 

> Ms. Johnson ________ buy that geography
> book.

① could not   ② might
③ should have   ④ will
⑤ is not going to

[7-9] 다음 중 어법상 <u>어색한</u> 문장을 고르시오.

07 

① He might have make a few mistakes.
② She could have called the police.
③ I used to live with several dogs.
④ You're not able to play basketball now.
⑤ No one can succeed all the time.

08

① We shouldn't tell these secrets to
   anyone.
② Were you able to find me among the
   crowd?
③ The soccer team would won all the
   game.
④ Alison and I still cannot agree on the
   topic.
⑤ Would you wait for me for a minute?

09 

① He used to break traffic laws before.
② The story he told me might be not true.
③ She couldn't find her friend in the market.
④ Mom just would not change her mind.
⑤ You won't succeed in school if you don't
   study.

[10-11] 주어진 문장과 의미가 같은 것을 고르시오.

10

> The bread in the oven might be delicious.

① The bread in the oven should not be delicious.

② The bread in the oven cannot be delicious.

③ The bread in the oven may be delicious.

④ The bread in the oven could have been delicious.

⑤ The bread in the oven used to be delicious.

11

> I used to listen to the radio on weekends.

① I could have listened to the radio on weekends.

② I might have listened to the radio on weekends.

③ I should listen to the radio on weekends.

④ I would listen to the radio on weekends.

⑤ I could listen to the radio on weekends.

[12-13] 빈칸에 들어갈 단어끼리 알맞게 짝지어진 것을 고르시오.

12

> A: __(A)__ you lend me some money?
> B: Okay, but __(B)__ you able to pay it back?

① Can – can   ② Would – could

③ Might – can   ④ Could – are

⑤ Should – are

13

> • That he has been to Rome __(A)__ be true.
> • Laura __(B)__ not going to go to bed early tonight.

① cannot – will   ② cannot – is

③ might have – is   ④ will – will

⑤ is – might

[14-15] 다음 밑줄 친 부분과 바꾸어 쓸 수 있는 것을 고르시오.

14

> You <u>may go</u> home if you finish your work.

① can go   ② should go

③ will go   ④ used to go

⑤ may have gone

15

> The alarm clock <u>might not have</u> gone off.

① could not have   ② may not have

③ must have   ④ should not have

⑤ used to have

[16-18] 주어진 우리말을 영어로 알맞게 옮긴 것을 고르시오.

16

> 홍수 때문에 나는 강을 건널 수가 없었다.

① I wouldn't cross the river due to the flood.

② I couldn't cross the river due to the flood.

③ I shouldn't cross the river due to the flood.

④ I used to cross the river due to the flood.

⑤ I might not cross the river due to the flood.

17

당신은 그 차를 타지 말았어야 했어요.

① You might not have taken the car.
② You must not have taken the car.
③ You shouldn't have taken the car.
④ You cannot have taken the car.
⑤ You couldn't have taken the car.

18

그 개울에는 물고기들이 많이 살곤 했었다.

① There must have been many fish in the stream.
② There should have been many fish in the stream.
③ There might be many fish in the stream.
④ There used to be many fish in the stream.
⑤ There could be many fish in the stream.

[19-21] 주어진 단어들을 바르게 배열하시오.

19 (the patient / have / could / saved)

→ The doctor ＿＿＿＿＿＿＿＿＿＿＿
if the patient had come earlier.

20 (change / our / are / to / bodies / able)

→ ＿＿＿＿＿＿＿＿＿＿＿＿＿
food into energy.

21 (used / Martha / live / to / with her family)

→ ＿＿＿＿＿＿＿＿＿＿＿ when
she was young.

[22-23] 어법상 틀린 부분을 찾아 바르게 고치시오.

22 ＿＿＿＿＿ → ＿＿＿＿＿

There used to been some difference of opinion between Julia and me, but now we are able to agree on almost anything.

23 ＿＿＿＿＿ → ＿＿＿＿＿

You should had paid back the money to your parents. You could have done some part-time jobs when you had a chance.

[24-25] 다음 글을 읽고 물음에 답하시오.

A: Mike, where are you going?
B: I have an appointment with my friend, Mom.
A: You (A) should finish the history report by tomorrow, or else your teacher is going to fail you.
B: But I have to get some game CDs from my friend today.
A: Well, then you ＿＿＿(B)＿＿＿ your report yesterday.

24 위 글의 (A) 대신 들어갈 수 있는 것은?

① are going to ② are able to ③ have to
④ used to ⑤ could

25 위 글의 (B)에 들어갈 말을 주어진 단어들을 사용하여 쓰시오.

→ ＿＿＿＿＿＿＿＿＿ (should, finish)

CHAPTER IV

to부정사와 동명사

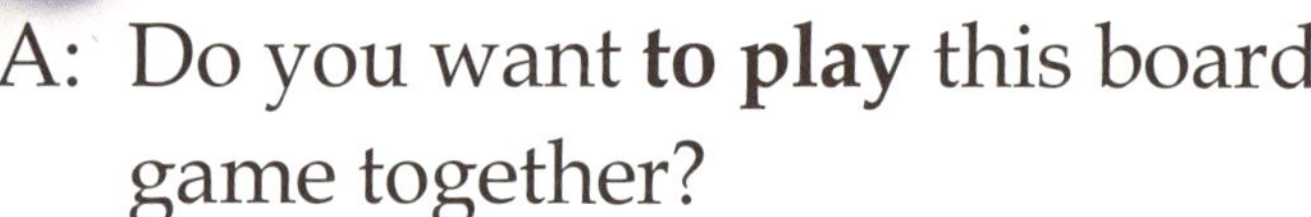

A: Do you want **to play** this board game together?

B : I want to but I don't know **how to** play it.

A: Don't worry. It's easy **to learn**.

to부정사의 쓰임

to부정사의 용법과 의미상의 주어

to부정사는 「to+동사원형」의 형태로, 명사·형용사·부사로 쓰입니다.

명사적 용법	**To eat** at night is not good for you. (주어) 밤에 먹는 것은 너에게 좋지 않아. He expected **not to fail** the test this year. (목적어) 그는 시험에 떨어지지 않길 기대했다. My plan is **to travel** around the world. (보어) 내 꿈은 세계를 여행하는 거야.
형용사적 용법	I don't have enough time **to hang** out with you. 너와 놀러 갈 시간이 없어.
부사적 용법	Jack turned on his computer **to finish** the work. (목적) Jack은 일을 끝내기 위해 그의 컴퓨터를 켰다. The little boy grew up **to be** president. (결과) 그 작은 소년은 자라서 대통령이 되었다. I was glad **to meet** him in the lobby. (감정의 원인) 로비에서 그를 만나게 되어 기뻤다.

「for+목적격」과 「of+목적격」이 to부정사의 의미상의 주어로 쓰입니다.

e.g. **It** is not good *for you* **to eat** at night. 밤에 먹는 것은 네에게 좋지 않아.

It's very nice *of you* **to say** so. (사람의 성격을 나타내는 형용사 +of) 네가 그렇게 말해 주다니 정말 친절하구나.

의문사 + to부정사

의문사 뒤에 to부정사를 써서 '~할지'를 뜻하는 명사구로 만들 수 있습니다.

what(명사)+to-V	무엇을 ~할지	how+to-V	어떻게 ~할지, ~하는 방법
when+to-V	언제 ~할지	which(명사)+to-V	어느 것을 ~할지
where+to-V	어디서 ~할지	whether+to-V	~할지 말지

e.g. I don't know **what to do** when I get back home. 나는 집으로 돌아오면 무엇을 해야 할지 모르겠다.

Please tell me **when to leave** this hotel tomorrow. 이 호텔을 내일 언제 떠나야 하는지 알려주세요.

She doesn't know **which color to choose** for her new shoes. 그녀는 새 신발로 어떤 색깔을 고를지 모른다.

I'm not sure **whether to wait** for him for another hour. 나는 그를 한 시간 더 기다릴지 말지 잘 모르겠다.

A   밑줄 친 to부정사의 역할에 동그라미 하시오.

01 I bent down <u>to pick</u> up the newspaper on the floor.   (명사 / 형용사 / 부사)

02 They wanted <u>to call</u> him and ask some questions.   (명사 / 형용사 / 부사)

03 <u>To study</u> animals in the wild seemed interesting to me.   (명사 / 형용사 / 부사)

04 You don't have permission <u>to enter</u> this building.   (명사 / 형용사 / 부사)

05 We stayed inside <u>to avoid</u> a heavy rain.   (명사 / 형용사 / 부사)

06 It was dangerous for me <u>to join</u> the air force at that time. (명사 / 형용사 / 부사)

07 Do you have some time <u>to go</u> to the gallery with me?   (명사 / 형용사 / 부사)

08 Her job is <u>to clean</u> windows outside high towers.   (명사 / 형용사 / 부사)

09 Farmers need enough water <u>to spray</u> on a field.   (명사 / 형용사 / 부사)

10 He went back to the building <u>to avoid</u> meeting his mom. (명사 / 형용사 / 부사)

B   주어진 말을 이용해 「의문사＋to부정사」 형태로 빈칸을 채우시오.

01 It's difficult to know _________________ when you grow up. (do, what)

02 No one told me _________________ this ice cream machine. (use, how)

03 I forgot _________________ the airplane back to my hometown. (take, when)

04 We should find out _________________ our mom's birthday. (celebrate, where)

05 She didn't know _________________ off the lamp. (turn, how)

06 Would you ask Jack _________________ this book or not? (buy, whether)

07 The students had no idea about _________________. (discuss, what)

08 He was not sure _________________ for her. (buy, which flower)

09 They haven't decided _________________ the dam or not. (build, whether)

10 I decided _________________ at the intersection. (go, way, which)

A 다음 세계 도시 별 여행 계획을 보고 빈칸에 알맞은 말을 쓰시오.

Cities I Want to Visit

Liverpool	watch soccer matches	Agra	take pictures of the Taj Mahal
Oslo	observe the beautiful aurora	Kathmandu	hike through the mountains
Naples	enjoy sunbathing	Moscow	enjoy cold weather

01 _______________________ in Liverpool is one of my dreams.

02 It must be fun _______________________ in Oslo.

03 I want _______________________ in Naples.

04 _______________________ in Moscow would be hard but fun.

05 In Agra, I would like _______________________.

06 It would be tiring _______________________ in Kathmandu, but I want to go there.

B 다음 글에서 밑줄 친 부분을 바르게 고치시오.

Several people helped **01** <u>protecting</u> Yellowstone National Park in the United States. In the 1600s and 1700s, some hunters went to the area to get some fur from animals. They came there **02** <u>to not harm</u> the beautiful place, so they spent several days there vewing its amazing features. Then they knew **03** <u>what do to</u> about it. When they returned to their towns, they told stories about the mountains. People wanted **04** <u>explored</u> Yellowstone, and Ferdinand Hayden, a photographer, and an artist went there **05** <u>capturing</u> the beauty of Yellowstone. They showed their pictures to Congress. President Grant had to decide **06** <u>to whether sign</u> a law, and he made Yellowstone America's first national park.

01 _______________   **02** _______________   **03** _______________

04 _______________   **05** _______________   **06** _______________

Actual Test

1 다음 밑줄 친 to부정사가 수식하는 말은?

> I have many things <u>to show</u> you in my room.

① have   ② many   ③ things
④ you   ⑤ in my room

2 다음 밑줄 친 부분과 용법이 같은 것은?

> He went outside <u>to take</u> some pictures of nature.

① You need <u>to wear</u> sunblock in summer.
② It is the best recipe <u>to make</u> lemon cookies.
③ I was going home <u>to take</u> a nap.
④ Do you have some time <u>to have</u> coffee?
⑤ <u>To eat</u> breakfast is important for teenagers.

3 다음 중 밑줄 친 부분의 용법이 <u>다른</u> 하나는?

① We don't have time <u>to waste</u>.
② I have some questions <u>to ask</u> you.
③ Please give me something <u>to drink</u>.
④ She often skips dinner <u>to lose</u> weight.
⑤ Do you have something <u>to say</u> to me?

4 다음 중 어법상 <u>어색한</u> 문장은?

① It is kind of you to help me with my luggage.
② We came here to not have a hard time.
③ Both Jack and Jill grew up to be teachers.
④ Mom was upset to see the messy room.
⑤ Do you know which train to take there?

5 빈칸에 들어갈 말이 알맞게 짝지어진 것은?

> • You can choose which ______(A)______ on TV.
> • Please tell me how __(B)__ back the money.

① watch to program – paying
② program to watch – to pay
③ watch program to – pay
④ program to watch – pay
⑤ watch program to – to pay

[6-7] 다음 밑줄 친 부분 중 어법상 <u>어색한</u> 것은?

6 My plan was <u>watch</u>① <u>a movie</u>② with him <u>this</u>③ weekend, but we <u>went</u>④ <u>to</u>⑤ a concert.

7 If you want <u>to</u>① <u>make</u>② new friends, you need <u>to</u>③ outgoing and <u>listen</u>④ <u>to</u>⑤ others.

[8-9] 다음 주어진 단어들을 바르게 배열하시오.

8 (happy / will / to / be / hear)

→ She _________________________ the news.

9 (to / think of / stopped / cross / to / how)

→ He _________________________ the road.

10 괄호 안의 동사를 알맞은 형태로 쓰시오.

> At summer camp, I did many things. First, I found the perfect spot (make) camp. After that, we went hiking. On the way, we stopped to pick some delicious berries.

→ _________________________

Learning a foreign language is fun.

I am fond of **talking** to foreigners.

How about you? Do you like **learning** a foreign language?

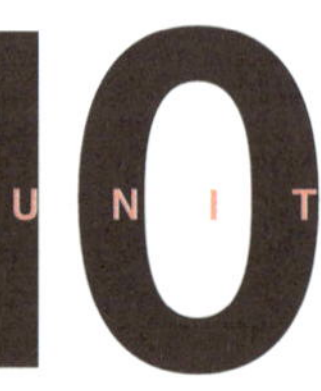

UNIT 10 동명사의 쓰임

동명사의 용법과 의미상의 주어

동명사는 「동사＋-ing」의 형태로, 문장에서 명사의 역할을 합니다. 동명사의 부정은 not이나 never를 동명사 앞에 써서 나타냅니다.

주어	**Standing** for a long time is hard for me. 오랫동안 서있는 것은 나에게 힘들다.
보어	His problem is **sleeping** too much. 그의 문제점은 잠을 너무 많이 잔다는 것이다.
타동사의 목적어	Do you *like* **raising** pets? 너는 애완 동물을 기르는 것을 좋아하니?
전치사의 목적어	I'm afraid *of* **speaking** in front of people. 나는 사람들 앞에서 말하는 것이 두렵다.
동명사의 부정	Her goal is **never putting** off her daily work. 그녀의 목표는 매일의 일을 절대 미루지 않는 것이다.

동명사가 나타내는 행위의 주체를 의미상의 주어라고 합니다. 문장의 주어와 동명사의 주어가 다를 때는 동명사 앞에 소유격을 써서 주어를 밝혀줍니다. 구어체에서는 목적격을 쓰기도 합니다.

문장의 주어＝동명사의 주어	*I* hate **being** late for class. 나는 (내가) 수업에 늦는 것이 싫다.
문장의 주어 ≠ 동명사의 주어	*I'm* sure of *his* **coming**. (소유격) 나는 그가 오는 것을 확신해. I can't stand *him* **smoking**. (목적격) 나는 그의 흡연을 참을 수가 없다.

동명사 표현

동명사를 포함하고 있는 주요 표현은 다음과 같습니다.

be used to + -ing	～하는 데 익숙하다	feel like + -ing	～하고 싶다
have difficulty + -ing	～하는 것이 어렵다	cannot help + -ing	～하지 않을 수 없다
look forward to + -ing	～하는 것을 기대하다	It is no use + -ing	～해도 소용없다
spend + 시간[돈] + (in) + -ing	～하는 데 시간[돈]을 쓰다	on + -ing	～하자마자

A 밑줄 친 동명사의 역할을 골라 동그라미 하시오.

01 <u>Raising</u> pets can be helpful for children. (주어 / 보어 / 목적어)

02 I like <u>jogging</u> early in the morning. (주어 / 보어 / 목적어)

03 George enjoyed <u>showing</u> his dogs to people. (주어 / 보어 / 목적어)

04 The only thing we can do is <u>waiting</u> for the police. (주어 / 보어 / 목적어)

05 Ava began <u>saving</u> money to buy new clothes. (주어 / 보어 / 목적어)

06 <u>Walking</u> a lot can be good exercise. (주어 / 보어 / 목적어)

07 Many people are interested in <u>making</u> money. (주어 / 보어 / 목적어)

08 The big issue is <u>decreasing</u> the company's debt. (주어 / 보어 / 목적어)

09 <u>Taking</u> a long drive makes people tired. (주어 / 보어 / 목적어)

10 Not <u>eating</u> enough vegetables is bad for your health. (주어 / 보어 / 목적어)

B 다음 밑줄 친 동명사의 의미상 주어에 동그라미 하시오.

01 I liked <u>seeing</u> my old friends.

02 He accepted my <u>cleaning</u> the garage as my weekend chore.

03 The athlete is good at <u>swimming</u> the backstroke.

04 I am thinking of <u>flying</u> jets as my career.

05 Uncle Sam enjoyed <u>catching</u> that large fish.

06 Doesn't she worry about his <u>coming</u> home after 10 p.m.?

07 The mosquitoes finally stopped <u>biting</u> me.

08 Does your father enjoy <u>fishing</u> in the river?

09 Nobody likes <u>cleaning</u> the bathroom.

10 Her mother is ashamed of Jenny's <u>learning</u> to dance.

A 다음 Lisa네 반 아이들의 특기와 취미를 보고 동명사를 사용하여 빈칸을 채우시오.

	good at …	enjoy …
Lisa	plant various trees	care for the plants in her garden
Jerry	sell his stuff at high prices	trade baseball cards
Maria	play the cello	fly kites at the park
Paul	write short stories	ride the roller coaster

01 Lisa is good at ________________________________ in her garden.

02 Lisa enjoys ________________________________.

03 ________________________________ is one thing that Jerry is good at.

04 Jerry's hobby is ________________________________.

05 Maria is proud of ________________________________ well.

06 ________________________________ is Maria's favorite hobby.

07 Paul is interested in ________________________________, and he writes them very well.

08 Paul often enjoys ________________________________ at the amusement park.

B 다음 글에서 주어진 동사를 알맞은 형태로 바꾸어 빈칸을 채우시오.

Yesterday, Aunt Jacobson felt like **01** ________(invite) her niece, Kelly, to her house. They were used to **02** ________(cook) together. Kelly looked forward to **03** ________(go) to her aunt's house after she got her call. On **04** ________(arrive) at her aunt's house, Kelly went to the kitchen. Her aunt was making chocolate cake and cookies. Kelly couldn't help **05** ________(pick) up some cookies that the aunt made. The aunt asked Kelly to mix the flour and egg well, but Kelly had difficulty **06** ________(mix) those two. The paste was too sweet, but it was no use **07** ________(add) more flour then. Finally, Kelly and her aunt finished cooking They had a good time together **08** ________(make) delicious cake and cookies.

Actual Test

1 다음 빈칸에 들어가기에 알맞은 것은?

> Many children don't enjoy ________ onions.

① eat　　② ate　　③ eaten
④ eating　　⑤ to eat

2 다음 밑줄 친 부분과 쓰임이 같은 것은?

> Jennifer began singing when she was three.

① Collecting stamps is my favorite hobby.
② Peeling onions makes people cry.
③ My plan was going to bed early.
④ Recycling is an important thing to do.
⑤ Jerry didn't remember dropping his book.

3 밑줄 친 동명사의 주어가 문장의 주어와 다른 것은?

① I enjoy taking long walks in the country.
② He likes his dog licking his hands.
③ Teachers should be good at speaking.
④ The scientist stopped doing the experiment.
⑤ The staff enjoyed meeting in the restaurant.

4 다음 중 어법상 어색한 것은?

① Calling a person too many times is not polite.
② People hate pushing in a long line.
③ Following not the rules is a serious problem.
④ My dog finally stopped barking.
⑤ Reading a lot improves your vocabulary.

[5-6] 다음 밑줄 친 부분 중 어법상 어색한 것은?

5 Gary's goal is become the best player
①　　②　　③
on his team, so he never stops practicing.
④　　⑤

6 Chewing gum can be fun, but some
①　　②
people hate listen to the sound of chewing
③　④　　⑤
gum.

7 주어진 우리말을 영어로 알맞게 옮긴 것은?

> 그녀는 그 고기를 먹지 않을 수 없었다.

① She couldn't eat the meat.
② She couldn't help eat but the meat.
③ She helped but eating the meat.
④ She couldn't help to eat the meat.
⑤ She couldn't help eating the meat.

[8-9] 다음 밑줄 친 부분을 바르게 고치시오.

8 Having not much fruit is bad for you.

→ ________________________________

9 You shouldn't spend your money buy unhealthy snacks.

→ ________________________________

10 주어진 단어들을 바르게 배열하시오.

> Jack was an animal trainer. However, he had never trained dolphins before. So, ____
> ________________________ (difficulty / was having / he / training) dolphins at the zoo.

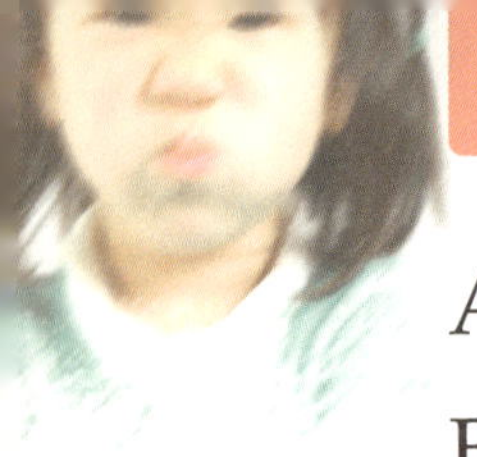

A: You **forgot to call** me on my birthday.

B : Really? But I **remember calling** you last night. Wasn't it your birthday yesterday?

A: No, it wasn't!

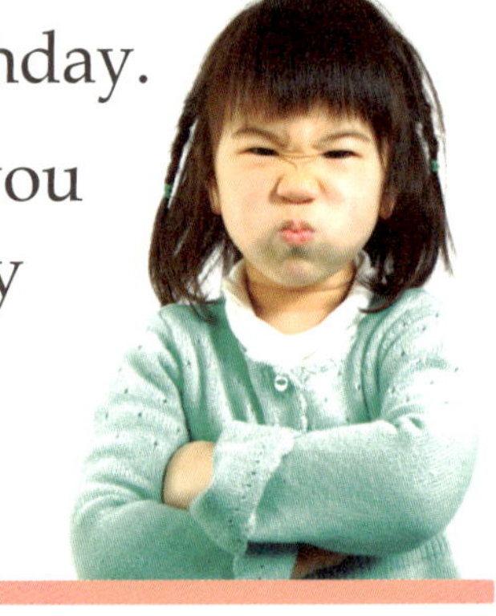

U N I T 11   to부정사와 동명사

to부정사와 동명사 목적어

동사 중에는 to부정사나 동명사만을 목적어로 취하는 동사가 있습니다.

동사＋to부정사	agree, choose, decide, expect, fail, hope, want, plan, promise, wish, etc.
동사＋동명사	avoid, consider, enjoy, finish, mind, give up, practice, imagine, etc.
동사＋to부정사/동명사	like, love, hate, start, begin, etc.

 I **decided to run** after him. 나는 그를 쫓아가기로 결심했다.

Do you **mind staying** here with me? 저와 여기 있는 게 싫으신가요?

Children **hate to eat** carrots. = Children **hate eating** carrots. 아이들은 당근 먹는 것을 싫어한다.

to부정사와 동명사 둘 다를 목적어로 취할 때 그 의미가 달라지는 동사가 있습니다.

remember / forget	Please **remember to lock** the door. (앞으로 할 일) 문을 잠글 것을 기억하세요. Do you **remember locking** the door? (과거에 했던 일) 너는 문을 잠근 것을 기억하니?
try	I **tried to open** the can, I failed. (노력) 나는 캔을 열려고 애썼지만, 실패했다. Everyone **tried opening** the can. (시도) 모두가 캔을 시험 삼아 열어보았다.
stop	The man **stopped to talk** to me. (목적) 그 남자는 나에게 말을 하기 위해 멈추었다. The man **stopped talking** to me. (진행 중인 일) 그 남자는 나에게 말하는 것을 멈추었다.

형용사 + to부정사 / 동명사

형용사와 함께 쓰이는 to부정사 또는 동명사 표현들이 있습니다.

be ready + to –V	～할 준비가 되다	be worth + -ing	～할 가치가 있다
be likely + to –V	～하기 쉽다	be busy + -ing	～하느라 바쁘다

 The athletes **are ready to run** their race. 선수들은 경주에 뛸 준비가 되었다.

The clerk **is busy making** coffee. 그 직원은 커피를 만드느라 바쁘다.

Check up 1

  괄호 안에서 알맞은 것을 고르시오.

01 The man decided (to join, joining) the army.

02 Do you mind (to answer, answering) the phone for us?

03 The car began (to move, moving) slowly along the street.

04 No one expected (to see, seeing) him at the meeting.

05 Some people hate (to watch, watching) horror movies.

06 You cannot give up (to speak, speaking) in front of class tomorrow.

07 House cats usually avoid (to go, going) outside.

08 The heavy rain started (to fall, falling).

  주어진 동사를 사용하여 문장을 완성하시오.

01 Children are likely ____________(feel) tired after 11 p.m.

02 The game was worth ____________(play) because it was very exciting.

03 I didn't agree ____________(show) you my homework.

04 My mom was busy ____________(cook) in the kitchen.

05 Most students are usually not ready ____________(take) tests.

06 I hoped ____________(be) alone at home, but no one else went out.

07 The girl finally finished ____________(talk) after an hour.

08 The man didn't plan ____________(go) out of town today.

09 The little girl started ____________(cry) in the toy store.

10 Do you enjoy ____________(jog) in the evening?

Check up 2

A　주어진 동사를 알맞은 형태로 바꾸어 대화를 완성하시오.

01 A: Did we lock the door before we left?

　　B: Yes, I remember ______________ the door. (lock)

02 A: Why is the baby crying so loudly?

　　B: I don't know. I tried ______________ her for one hour, but I failed. (calm)

03 A: Look! An earthquake hit the country!

　　B: What a disaster! Let's stop ______________ to the news. (listen)

04 A: Oh, we have two packs of eggs in the cart.

　　B: Sorry, I forgot ______________ one in the cart already. (put)

05 A: We're short of popcorn and soda.

　　B: I'll go get some more. Let's stop ______________ the movie for a second. (watch)

B　다음 글에서 밑줄 친 부분을 바르게 고치시오. 맞으면 O로 표시하시오.

I am a forester, and I like **01** work in woods. I started **02** hike when I was young, and I loved **03** being in the forest. Then, I decided **04** taking care of forests for my job. I usually finish **05** to work before the night falls. But I work late from time to time, because some loggers try **06** to avoid me and plan **07** cutting down trees at night. Sometimes I don't mind **08** cut trees down because that keeps the forest healthy. But the loggers must follow laws that protect the environment.

01 ______________　　02 ______________　　03 ______________

04 ______________　　05 ______________　　06 ______________

07 ______________　　08 ______________

Actual Test

[1-2] 다음 빈칸에 들어가기에 알맞은 것은?

1

> It was difficult _____ him to stay awake late at night.

① in　　② of　　③ for　　④ at　　⑤ on

2

> It was foolish _____ me to call you them.

① in　　② of　　③ by　　④ at　　⑤ on

3 다음 빈칸에 들어갈 수 <u>없는</u> 것은?

> I _______ reading an English newspaper.

① enjoyed　　② started　　③ finished
④ gave up　　⑤ decided

4 다음 밑줄 친 부분 중 어법상 <u>어색한</u> 것은?

① Would you <u>mind turning</u> down the volume?
② You're not <u>ready to work</u> at this company.
③ The strong wind <u>began to blow</u> in the desert.
④ I didn't <u>expect to have</u> dinner at this café.
⑤ Did you consider <u>to join</u> our book club?

5 다음 대화의 빈칸에 알맞은 것은?

> **A:** Do you remember _______ bicycles along the beach last summer?
> **B:** Of course, I do. We really had a good time back then.

① rode　　② ride　　③ rides
④ to ride　　⑤ riding

[6-7] 다음 밑줄 친 부분 중 어법상 <u>어색한</u> 것은?

6 I really like <u>to ski</u>, so I hope <u>visiting</u> a ski
①　　　　　　　　　②
resort <u>near</u> <u>my</u> hometown and enjoy <u>skiing</u>
③　④　　　　　　　　　　　⑤
there.

7 A: Please <u>stop shaking</u> your legs. You're
①
<u>making</u> me <u>uncomfortable</u>.
②　　　③
B: Sorry, but I just cannot stop <u>to shake</u> legs
④
when <u>I'm nervous</u>.
⑤

[8-9] 다음 문장에서 어법상 <u>어색한</u> 부분을 고쳐 다시 쓰시오.

8 You should not avoid to talk to your parents.

→ _______________________________

9 Pets are worth to raise with children.

→ _______________________________

10 주어진 단어들을 바르게 배열하여 문장을 완성하시오.

> Global warming is changing our climate and the lives of all living things on Earth. Big ice in the Arctic area is melting, and sea levels are rising. Someday, some islands might disappear! We should (to / try / start / do something / to).

→ We should _______________________.

Review Test

[1-3] 다음 빈칸에 들어가기에 알맞은 것은?

 **01**

> The man had many friends _______ to his birthday party.

① invite   ② invites   ③ invited
④ inviting   ⑤ to invite

 **02**

> All the students in the stands were busy _______ for their teams.

① cheer   ② cheers   ③ cheered
④ cheering   ⑤ to cheer

 **03**

> I'll show you how _______ the problem.

① solve   ② solves   ③ solved
④ solving   ⑤ to solve

[4-5] 다음 빈칸에 들어갈 수 없는 것은?

 **04**

> It's very _______ of him to say that.

① stupid   ② easy   ③ wise
④ kind   ⑤ foolish

05

> I'm not sure _______ to fix the chair.

① what   ② how   ③ when
④ where   ⑤ whether

[6-7] 다음 밑줄 친 부분이 어법상 어색한 것은?

 **06**

① He couldn't help <u>laughing</u> loudly.
② No one looked forward to <u>going</u> on a picnic.
③ I felt like crying after <u>watching</u> the movie.
④ We had difficulty <u>choosing</u> the best film.
⑤ Babies are likely <u>being</u> in danger.

 **07**

① <u>To feed</u> a pet can be annoying.
② Who <u>wants to go</u> to a zoo?
③ It was easy <u>for her to ring</u> the bell above.
④ The man <u>is used to eat</u> alone.
⑤ The little girl <u>grew up to be</u> beautiful.

[8-9] 다음 중 어법상 어색한 문장을 고르시오.

 **08**

① He was pleased to see her again.
② Don't spend your time watching TV.
③ The woman was not ready to go out.
④ It is no use regret your mistakes.
⑤ It is worth traveling all over the world.

09

① She hopes to study music at the university.
② I decided to raise some plants at home.
③ You shouldn't give up to learn the piano.
④ My father always wished to have a daughter.
⑤ The cook failed to please the customer.

10

① I felt like to go home right away.

② We were used to have dinner at 5.

③ The new film is worth to watch.

④ I'm looking forward to seeing her.

⑤ She is busy to prepare her lunch.

11

① I agree visit the post office first.

② Don't expect tasting delicious dish here.

③ He didn't plan buying a new smart phone.

④ I practiced diving from the springboard.

⑤ Would you promise not telling a secret?

12

① Did you have any difficulty to come here?

② I hated being at home alone.

③ She gave up to drink for a month.

④ I spent 30 dollars to buy the necklace.

⑤ She couldn't help to go to the bathroom.

13 짝지어진 두 문장의 의미가 같은 것을 고르시오.

① He tried going to bed early.
   He tried to go to bed early.

② Did you remember to water the plant?
   Did you remember watering the plant?

③ My brother likes to collect bugs.
   My brother likes collecting bugs.

④ Don't forget to turn off the TV.
   Don't forget turning off the TV.

⑤ Everyone tried to open the glass box.
   Everyone tried opening the glass box.

14

> **A:** Have you enjoyed __(A)__ around this island?
>
> **B:** Yes. I'll always remember __(B)__ along the beach.

① traveling – walks   ② to travel – walking

③ to travel – to walk   ④ traveling – walking

⑤ traveling – to walk

15

> • I hoped __(A)__ to my English teacher about my worries.
> • On __(B)__ him, she tried to run away.

① to talk – see   ② to talk – to see

③ to talk – seeing   ④ talking – seeing

⑤ talking – to see

16

> 그는 화장실을 청소해야 할지 말지 몰랐다.

① He didn't know how to clean the bathroom.

② He didn't know when to clean the bathroom.

③ He didn't know where to clean the bathroom.

④ He didn't know which to clean the bathroom.

⑤ He didn't know whether to clean the bathroom.

17

잠을 적게 자는 것은 내 건강에 좋지 않다.

① It is not healthy for me sleeping less.
② It is unhealthy for me to sleep less.
③ It is unhealthy of me to sleep less.
④ It is unhealthy of me sleeping less.
⑤ It is unhealthy of my sleeping less.

18

사람들은 여름에 화상을 입기가 쉽다.

① People are likely getting sunburn in summer.
② People likely to get sunburn in summer.
③ People likely getting sunburn in summer.
④ People are likely get sunburn in summer.
⑤ People are likely to get a sunburn in summer.

[19-21] 주어진 단어들을 바르게 배열하시오.

19 (the abandoned / to / tried / enter / house)

→ No one _______________

_______________________.

20 (to / need / consider / what / do / to)

→ We _______________________ at the camp site.

21 (his time / to / hope / doing nothing / spend)

→ Andy doesn't _______________________

_______________________.

[22-23] 어법상 틀린 부분을 찾아 바르게 고치시오.

22

It is difficult of my mom to make different dishes for us every day.

_______________ → _______________

23

My sister and I planned go abroad for the summer vacation, but it was too expensive.

_______________ → _______________

[24-25] 다음 글을 읽고 물음에 답하시오.

Maria lives in La Laguna, Mexico. Each January, the gray whales arrive near La Laguna (A) to stay for three months. Then they go farther north for the summer. Whale watchers, scientists, and photographers visit La Laguna from all over the world to observe the whales. (B) (with / communicate / the whales / to) can be fun and exciting. Maria herself enjoys watching whales every day!

24 다음 밑줄 친 부분 중 (A)와 쓰임이 같은 것은?

① People rode a boat to watch the whale.
② She wants to see small dolphins.
③ No one expected to meet whales in sea.
④ To watch whales can be interesting.
⑤ It is dangerous to play with the whales.

25 위 글의 밑줄 친 (B)를 바르게 배열하시오.

→ _______________________

분사구문

Listening to the music, I walked along the street.

Walking along the street, I saw my friends.

Talking to my friend, I met my mom.

12

분사구문의 형태와 쓰임

분사구문의 기본 용법

분사구문은 종속절로 쓰인 부사절을 부사구로 바꾸어 표현하는 형태로, 시간·이유·양보·조건·부대상황 등을 나타냅니다. 부사절의 주어가 주절의 주어와 같을 때는, 부사절의 주어를 없애고 동사를 현재분사(동사원형 + -ing)으로 바꾸어 만듭니다.

종속절	주절
~~Because he arrived~~ early at the airport, ⤷ **Arriving** (분사) = **Arriving** early at the airport,	**he** had enough time to have a big lunch. (주절의 주어 = 종속절의 주어)

 **Finishing(= After he finished)** his work, he called his parents. (시간)
나는 얼굴을 씻은 후에, 샤워를 했다.

Having(= Because I had) failed to enter college, I had to go abroad to study. (이유)
대학 입학에 실패했기 때문에, 나는 유학을 떠나야만 했다.

Waking(= Although he woke) up early, he couldn't see the sunrise. (양보)
그는 일찍 일어났음에도 불구하고, 일출을 볼 수 없었다.

Reaching(= If you reach) the end of this road, you will see a gas station. (조건)
이 길의 끝에 다다르면, 주유소를 볼 수 있을 것입니다.

Eating(= As he ate) dinner, Sam watched his favorite TV show. (부대상황)
저녁을 먹으면서, Sam은 가장 좋아하는 TV 프로그램을 시청했다.

분사구문의 부정형

분사구문의 앞에 not이나 never를 붙여 분사구문의 부정을 나타냅니다.

 **Because she wasn't** fond of math at all, **she** always fell asleep in math class.
= **Not being** fond of math at all, she always fell asleep in math class.
그녀는 수학을 전혀 좋아하지 않았기 때문에, 수학 시간에는 항상 잠에 빠져들었다.

As he has never taken an English class before, **he** doesn't know the alphabet.
= **Never having** taken an English class before, he doesn't know the alphabet.
전에 영어 수업을 들어본 적이 없기 때문에, 그는 알파벳을 모른다.

A 밑줄 친 부분을 분사구문으로 바꾸어 쓰시오.

01 After they finished eating the main course, everybody ate dessert.

→ _________________________, everybody ate dessert.

02 If you keep driving north, you might come to a crossroad.

→ _________________________, you might come to a crossroad.

03 As she picked the strawberries, Maria sang a song.

→ _________________________, Maria sang a song.

04 As she sat on the airplane, Jane watched outside the window.

→ _________________________, Jane watched outside the window.

05 Although we hurried to get to the station, we couldn't catch the train.

→ _________________________, we couldn't catch the train.

06 Because she did not want to be late for the class, she started to run fast.

→ _________________________, she started to run fast.

B 다음 문장의 분사구문을 부사절로 바꾸어 쓰시오.

01 Reading a book, I turn off my cell phone.

→ When _________________________, I turn off my cell phone.

02 Knowing the answer to the question, Jay didn't raise his hand.

→ Although _________________________, Jay didn't raise his hand.

03 Not having many chances to meet foreigners, Mr. Kim isn't good at English.

→ Because _________________________, Mr. Kim isn't good at English.

04 Spending all of his paycheck, he didn't have any more money.

→ Since _________________________, he didn't have any more money.

05 Not being ready for the trip, I forgot to pack my toothbrush.

→ As _________________________, I forgot to pack my toothbrush.

06 Opening his new business, Bob quit his job.

→ Before _________________________, Bob quit his job.

Check up 2

A 학생들이 지각한 이유를 적은 표를 보고 분사구문으로 빈칸을 채우시오.

	Tuesday	Wednesday
Sunny	failed to catch the bus	not late: woke up early
Jamie	not able to hear the alarm	not late: rode in his father's car
Jennifer	argued with her mom	spent too much time choosing clothes

01 ________________________________, Sunny was late on Tuesday.

02 ________________________, Sunny was not late for school on Wednesday.

03 ________________________________, Jamie was late on Tuesday.

04 ____________________________, Jamie came to school on time Wednesday.

05 __________________________, Jennifer couldn't make it on time on Tuesday.

06 ________________________________, Jennifer was late again on Wednesday.

B 다음 글에서 밑줄 친 부분을 분사구문으로 바꾸어 쓰시오.

Last weekend, **01** because he felt bored, Eric went to travel through a swamp. The driver of the boat started to slow down **02** as he entered the swamp. **03** Since the swamp looked dark, it made Eric a little nervous. **04** As he didn't know what kinds of things could be hiding in the dark water, he felt afraid. **05** As moss hanged from their branches, the trees around the swamp looked like spider webs. All of a sudden, he heard a loud splash. **06** Although he looked around, he saw nothing in the water. **07** After he heard another splash, he came much closer to the water. **08** When he shined his flashlight out into the darkness, he saw the tail of an alligator.

01 ________________________

02 ________________________

03 ________________________

04 ________________________

05 ________________________

06 ________________________

07 ________________________

08 ________________________

Actual Test

1 다음 빈칸에 들어가기에 알맞은 것은?

> ________________________, I felt very excited.

① Before I riding the roller coaster
② Before rode the roller coaster
③ To ride the roller coaster
④ Ride the roller coaster
⑤ Riding the roller coaster

[2-3] 다음 밑줄 친 부분과 바꾸어 쓸 수 있는 것은?

2

> As he read the newspaper, he had breakfast.

① Read　　② Reads　　③ To read
④ Reading　　⑤ Be reading

3

> Since Mr.Kim is generous, he forgives any of
> our mistakes.

① Since is generous　　② Is generous
③ Generous is　　④ Being generous
⑤ Generous Mr.Kim

4 주어진 우리말을 영어로 알맞게 옮긴 것은?

> 음악을 들으면서 Jay는 조깅을 하러 갔다.

① Listening to the music, Jay goes jogging.
② Listen to the music, Jay went jogging.
③ Jay went jogging, listening to the music.
④ Jay goes jogging, listen to the music.
⑤ While goes jogging, Jay listens to the
music.

[5-6] 다음 밑줄 친 부분 중 어법상 어색한 것은?

5 Ridden a horse, he watched a beautiful
　　①　　　　　　　②
sunset. Being excited at the sunset, he stopped.
　　　　③　　　　　　④　　　　　　　⑤

6 Being afraid of water, she cannot swim.
　　①　　　②
Liking never water, she prefers mountains.
　③　　　　　　　④　　　⑤

7 다음 밑줄 친 부분을 부사절로 알맞게 고친 것은?

> Seeing my father, the cat ran away from him.

① Although the cat saw my father
② Although the cat sees my father
③ When the cat didn't see my father
④ When the cat sees my father
⑤ When the cat saw my father

[8-9] 다음 밑줄 친 부사절을 분사구문으로 고치시오.

8 After I checked the time, I caught the taxi.

→ ________________________________

9 Because she was not hungry, Jane
skipped dinner.

→ ________________________________

10 다음 글의 밑줄 친 단어들을 바르게 배열하시오.

> People don't know much about wolves.
> Believing that wolves kill and eat humans,
> people are afraid of them. However, (their /
> eating / for / meals / meat), they hardly ever
> hurt people.

→ ________________________________

While driving, Ellie got a call from her friend.

With her friend talking to her, she kept driving.

It raining hard, she stopped driving for a minute.

13 다양한 분사구문

접속사 + 분사구문

분사구문의 의미를 명확히 나타내기 위해, 종속접속사를 분사구문 앞에 함께 쓸 수 있습니다. 주로 시간·양보를 나타내는 접속사를 분사구문 앞에 써 줍니다. 단, **because**는 분사구문 앞에 쓸 수 없습니다.

e.g. **After washing(= After I washed)** my face, I took a shower. 나는 얼굴을 씻은 후에 샤워를 했다.
Although leaving(= Although he left) home years ago, he still misses his family every day. 수 년 전에 집을 떠났음에도 불구하고, 그는 아직도 매일 그의 가족을 그리워한다.

with + 분사구문

분사구문 앞에 「with + 목적어」를 붙여 '(목적어가) ~한 채로, ~하면서' 라는 부대상황을 나타냅니다.

e.g. **With her dog sleeping** beside her, she kept reading. 그녀의 개가 옆에서 자고 있는 채로, 그녀는 책을 읽었다.
With his hair cut by the barber, he couldn't stop crying.
이발사에 의해 머리가 짧게 잘리면서, 그는 울음을 멈출 수가 없었다.

분사구문의 주어

분사구문의 주어가 주절의 주어와 같지 않을 때 분사구문 앞에 주어를 따로 표시합니다.

종속절	주절
~~Because~~ it snowed heavily, → **It snowing** heavily,	**we** stayed home today. (종속절의 주어 ≠ 주절의 주어)

e.g. **As there was** a tall building in front of my house, **I** couldn't enjoy sunlight at home.
= **There being** a tall building in front of my house, **I** couldn't enjoy sunlight at home.
집 앞에 높은 건물이 있었기 때문에, 나는 집에서 햇빛을 즐길 수가 없었다.

분사구문의 주어가 불특정한 사람(we, they, people, you)을 가리킬 때는 주절의 주어와 다르더라도 주어를 표시하지 않으며, 이를 비인칭 독립분사구문이라고 합니다.

Frankly speaking	솔직히 말해서	Generally speaking	일반적으로 말해서
Strictly speaking	엄밀히 말하자면	Considering (that) ~	~를 생각하자면

A 주어진 단어들을 바르게 배열하여 분사구문을 만드시오.

01 (to the mall / walking / while), I ran into an old friend of mine.

→ _________________________________, I ran into an old friend of mine.

01 (hurting / at the football game / since / his back), Alex stayed at the hospital.

→ _________________________________, Alex stayed at the hospital.

03 (his short hair / blowing / with / in the wind), he stood on the hill for a while.

→ _________________________________, he stood on the hill for a while.

04 (how cold it was / hearing / outside / after), I decided not to go out.

→ _________________________________, I decided not to go out.

05 (both / legs / its / with / broken), the bird could not fly.

→ _________________________________, the bird could not fly.

06 (being / good at public speaking / although), he couldn't say a word at the meeting.

→ _________________________________, he couldn't say a word at the meeting.

B 밑줄 친 부사절을 분사구문으로 바꾸시오.

01 As Joe finished dinner, the telephone rang.

→ _________________________________, the telephone rang.

02 Before the waiter came to our table, I already had decided to eat beef.

→ _________________________________, I already had decided to eat beef.

03 While Jack tried to sleep last night, a mosquito kept buzzing in his ear.

→ _________________________________, a mosquito kept buzzing in his ear.

04 As it rains a lot in summer, I always carry an umbrella.

→ _________________________________, I always carry an umbrella.

05 Although Sarah said hello to him, the man didn't recognize Sarah.

→ _________________________________, the man didn't recognize Sarah.

06 Because there was no one at home, I made breakfast myself.

→ _________________________________, I made breakfast myself.

A   각 사람이 보내려고 하는 구호품 목록을 보고 분사구문을 사용해 빈칸을 채우시오.

What You Want to Send to the Disaster Area

	Item	Reason		Item	Reason
I	blankets	it is cold there	Paul	flashlights	there is no electricity
Tom	soap	people need to get clean	Ellie	canned food	there are people who are hungry
Susan	books	there are children who need to study	Sam	bottled water	people need some clean water

01 ________________________, I'll send some blankets to the area.

02 ________________________, Tom wishes to send soap to them.

03 ________________________, Susan will send books.

04 ________________________, Paul wants to send flashlights to the area.

05 ________________________, Ellie will send canned food.

06 ________________________, Sam will send them bottled water.

B   알맞은 분사구문을 골라 글을 완성하시오.

being the first people	strictly speaking	it being sunny	being outside
when having free time	although starting	considering that	being young

Everyone knows that the Wright brothers made an airplane. **01**________
________, their airplane is not the same as that of today. However,
02______________ they made the first airplane, we should thank
them. **03**______________, the brothers enjoyed playing with helicopter
toys. **04**______________, they flew high-flying kites. **05**______________
a printing business to make money, they never forgot about flying.
06______________, they researched past inventions. **07**______________
________, the brothers always went outside to do experiments. Finally,
08______________ who made an airplane, they flew their homemade
aircraft on a historic day in 1903.

Actual Test

[1-2] 다음 빈칸에 들어가기에 알맞은 것은?

1

> ________, I will go out to ride my bike.

① Being the weather nice
② Being the weather is nice
③ When the weather nice
④ The weather being nice
⑤ The weather is nice

2

> With her hands ________ together, the girl prayed before she slept.

① hold　　② holds　　③ held
④ holding　　⑤ to hold

3 다음 중 어법상 <u>어색한</u> 문장은?

① It being dark, all the children went home.
② While having dinner, we watched TV.
③ Being sleepy, the cat closed his eyes.
④ Speaking generally, girls like flowers.
⑤ Considering that he's an adult, I can't understand his mistake.

4 다음 빈칸에 들어갈 말이 알맞게 짝지어진 것은?

> - ___(A)___ late for work, she took a taxi.
> - ___(B)___ getting hot, the bear went into the cage.

① It – It　　　② It – Because
③ Being – Being　　④ Being – It
⑤ Because – The bear

5 주어진 우리말을 영어로 알맞게 옮긴 것은?

> 의자를 고치고 난 후, 그는 샤워를 했다.

① After he fix the chair, he took a shower.
② After he fixing the chair, he took a shower.
③ After fix the chair, he took a shower.
④ After fixing the chair, he took a shower.
⑤ Him fixing the chair, he took a shower.

[6-7] 다음 밑줄 친 부분 중 어법상 <u>어색한</u> 것은?

6 With tears fell down his face, the soldier
　　　①　　　②　　　③
ran to hug his son.
④　　⑤

7 Snowing hard, the doctor went outside
　　①
to visit his patient. After finishing seeing his
　　②　　　　　　　③　　　④
patient, he hurried back to his house.
　　　　　⑤

[8-9] 다음 밑줄 친 부사절을 분사구문으로 고치시오.

8 <u>Because I was tired,</u> I went home early.

→ ________________, I went home early.

9 <u>As there is a tall tower,</u> people enjoy the night view there.

→ ________________, people enjoy the night view there.

10 다음 글에서 밑줄 친 부분을 바르게 고치시오.

> I enjoy watching TV programs about animals. <u>There is fun stories,</u> the programs also show sad stories about abandoned pets.

→ ________________

Review Test

[1-3] 다음 빈칸에 들어가기에 알맞은 것은?

01

> Not _______ hard, you might fail the test.

① study　　② studies　　③ studying
④ to study　⑤ studied

02

> With its top _______ with snow, the mountain stood high.

① cover　　② covers　　③ covering
④ to cover　⑤ covered

03

> _______ that you have difficulty waking up, you should go to bed early.

① Consider　　　② Considers
③ Considering　④ To consider
⑤ Considered

[4-5] 다음 두 문장을 한 문장으로 만들때, 빈칸에 알맞은 말을 고르시오.

04

> I took the subway to school. I met Peter.
> = _______ the subway to school, I met Peter.

① Although taking　② When taking
③ Because taking　④ If taking
⑤ Since taking

05

> The soap was slippery. I dropped the soap.
> = _______ slippery, I dropped it.

① It being　　　② Since being
③ The soap being　④ Being
⑤ The soap is

[6-7] 다음 밑줄 친 부분이 어법상 어색한 것을 고르시오.

06

① <u>Not having</u> any job, he couldn't pay his bills.
② <u>Reaching</u> the next stop, the bus slowed down.
③ <u>Never having</u> a girlfriend, he was lonely.
④ <u>Reading</u> the book, I fell asleep quickly.
⑤ <u>Being</u> too sunny, you should wear a cap.

07

① <u>Tom finishing</u> breakfast, I washed the dishes.
② <u>While listening</u> to the music, I was jogging.
③ <u>Because dark</u> in the room, I turned on the light.
④ <u>After touching</u> a cat, she sneezed hard.
⑤ <u>After becoming</u> famous, Lisa didn't call me.

08 

As <u>Jean loves math</u>, the question was easy to her.

① Jean loving math   ② Jean loves math
③ As loving math   ④ Loving math
⑤ Loving Jean math

09 

<u>Since Lisa had never taken an airplane</u>, she got frightened.

① Having taken an airplane
② Since taking an airplane
③ Never taking an airplane
④ Never having taken an airplane
⑤ Lisa never taken having an airplane

[10-12] 다음 빈칸에 들어가기에 알맞은 것을 고르시오.

10 

The woman was sitting on the bench with her legs _________.

① cross   ② crosses   ③ crossed
④ to cross   ⑤ crossing

11

Strictly _________, dolphins are not fish because they breathe air.

① speak   ② speaks   ③ spoke
④ spoken   ⑤ speaking

12

_________ unable to buy a car, she bought a bicycle.

① Be   ② Is   ③ Been
④ To be   ⑤ Being

13 다음 각 문장을 분사구문으로 <u>잘못</u> 고친 것은?

① After working 25 years, my father retired.
→ Working 25 years, my father retired.

② Because it's foggy, drive carefully.
→ Being foggy, drive carefully.

③ Since he broke his legs, he couldn't move.
→ Breaking his legs, he couldn't move.

④ When his mom went out, Jack just slept.
→ His mom going out, Jack just slept.

⑤ Before he became president, Peter was a salesman.
→ Before becoming president, Peter was a salesman.

[14-15] 빈칸에 들어갈 말이 알맞게 짝지어진 것을 고르시오.

14

• _(A)_ a vegetarian, Tess doesn't eat meat.
• With her hair _(B)_ red, she got a lot of attention.

① It being – dyeing   ② Being – dyed
③ Tess being – dyed   ④ Being – dyeing
⑤ Tess being – dyeing

15

- (A) ______ going to bed, I always brush my teeth.
- (B) ______ staying in Japan, I traveled to Tokyo.

① Before – Though   ② Though – While
③ And – Though   ④ Before – While
⑤ Though – Before

[16-18] 주어진 우리말을 영어로 알맞게 옮긴 것을 고르시오.

16

오늘은 공휴일이므로 나는 학교에 가지 않았다.

① Since a holiday, I didn't go to school.
② It was a holiday, I didn't go to school.
③ Since being a holiday, I didn't go to school.
④ Being a holiday, I didn't go to school.
⑤ It being a holiday, I didn't go to school.

17

그녀가 책을 좋아한다는 것을 생각해 보면, 그녀는 도서관에 있을 것이다.

① It considers she likes books, she'll be at the library.
② She liking the book, she'll be at the library.
③ Liking the book, she'll be at the library.
④ Considering liking books, she'll be at the library.
⑤ Considering she likes books, she'll be at the library.

18

물을 마시지 않아서 나는 목이 말랐다.

① Not drinking water, I was thirsty.
② Drinking not water, I was thirsty.
③ Being not drinking water, I was thirsty.
④ I not drinking water, I was thirsty.
⑤ Drinking water not, I was thirsty.

[19-20] 밑줄 친 분사구문을 부사절로 바꾸어 쓰시오.

19

Talking to you, I understood the answer.

→ After ________________, I understood the answer.

20

Not wanting to hurt her feelings, Sam didn't tell her the bad news.

→ Since ________________________, Sam didn't tell her the bad news.

21 다음 글에서 어법상 어색한 곳을 찾아 바르게 고치시오.

Today's soccer game was fun, ①being full of action! Tina ②sent the ball to Michael, ③kicked it too hard. Tina's kick made the ball go out of bounds. Jackie, on the other team, threw the ball hard, almost ④scoring a goal. Andre, the goal keeper, ⑤jumping to the side, blocked it. He kicked it back into the field.

________ → ________

CHAPTER VI

수동태

English is spoken everywhere in the world.

It is used for many purposes: business, research, and so on.

14 UNIT 수동태의 용법

수동태의 기본 용법

수동태는 주어가 '~되다(당하다)'라는 수동의 의미를 나타내며, 「주어(대상)＋be동사＋p.p.」의 형태를 갖습니다.

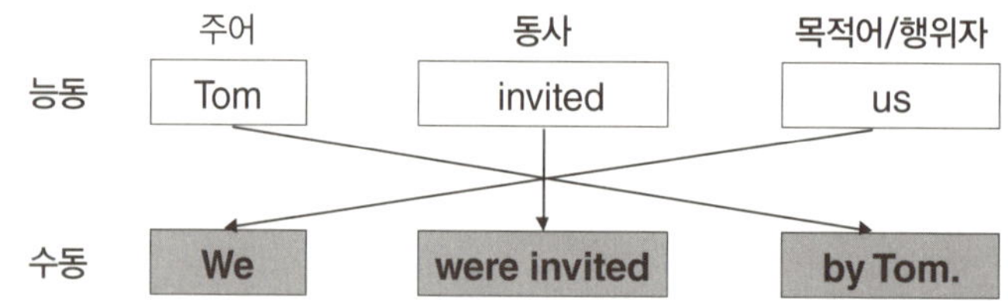

e.g. This soup **was not made by** my mom. 이 수프는 우리 엄마가 만든 것이 아니다.

The newspaper **is delivered** every morning. 신문은 매일 아침 배달된다.

4형식 · 5형식 문장의 수동태

목적어가 2개인 4형식 문장은 2가지 형태의 수동태를 만들 수 있습니다. 목적어와 목적격보어가 있는 5형식 문장에서는 목적어만 수동태 문장의 주어로 쓰일 수 있습니다.

4형식	They give *me presents* every Christmas. (간접목적어 + 직접목적어) 그들은 크리스마스마다 나에게 선물을 준다. → *I am given presents* every Christmas. (간접목적어가 주어) → *Presents are given (to) me* every Christmas. (직접목적어가 주어) (직접목적어가 주어로 쓰인 경우 간접목적어 앞에 쓰인 to나 for 생략 가능)
5형식	목적어 + 목적격 보어(명사) People elected *Mr.Kim president* again. 사람들은 Mr. Kim을 또 대통령으로 뽑았다. → *Mr. Kim* **was elected** president by people. (O) → President was elected Mr. Kim by people. (X)
	지각동사나 사역동사의 목적격 보어로 쓰인 동사원형은 to부정사로 바뀝니다. Our teacher will **make** us *clean* the lab. 우리 선생님은 우리에게 실험실을 청소하라고 시킬 것이다. → We will **be made *to clean*** the lab.

A 괄호 안에서 알맞은 것을 고르시오.

01 Waitresses and waiters (serve, are served by) customers.

02 Ann (handed, was handed) a menu at the restaurant.

03 In the car accident, both of his parents (killed, were killed).

04 The teacher (explained, was explained) the lesson to the students.

05 The picture (did not draw, wasn't drawn) by my brother.

06 A hurricane (destroyed, was destroyed) the small village in a day.

07 The new building (built, was built) a week ago.

08 I (told, was told) to be here at 8:30 in the morning.

09 These shoes and pants (made, were made) in China.

10 The mail (did not deliver, was not delivered) this morning.

B 밑줄 친 부분을 바르게 고치시오.

01 The message <u>was receiving by</u> Tom in your office. → ____________

02 The musical <u>was perform by</u> only three actresses. → ____________

03 A lot of rice <u>is grows</u> in East Asia. → ____________

04 The farmer's wagon <u>pulled by</u> two horses. → ____________

05 The cell phone <u>was turning off</u>. → ____________

06 That book <u>was sell</u> out in many countries. → ____________

07 A bill <u>was sent me to</u> at the end of the month. → ____________

08 The army <u>surrounded by</u> the enemy an hour ago. → ____________

09 Ken <u>was invited not</u> to your party. → ____________

10 I was made <u>wash</u> the dog. → ____________

Check up 2

A   학생들의 청소 분담표를 보고 주어진 동사를 활용하여 문장을 완성하시오.

Keeping the Class Clean

Name	Area	Tool	Help
Inho	windows	window cleaner	x
Bora	floor	mop, basket	asking Sam for help
Sam	all the desks	a cloth	helping Bora
Sumi	blackboard	blackboard eraser	x

01 The windows ____________ by Inho. (clean)

02 Inho ____________ a window cleaner for cleaning the windows. (need)

03 Sumi ____________ the blackboard with a blackboard eraser. (clean)

04 A mop and basket ____________ to clean the floor. (use)

05 Bora ____________ by Sam to clean the floor. (help)

06 Sam ____________ help to Bora to clean the floor. (give)

07 The blackboard ____________ by Sam. He's in charge of all the desks. (wipe, not)

08 Bora ______________ the floor of the classroom. (make, clean)

B   주어진 동사를 능동태 또는 수동태로 바꾸어 글을 완성하시오.

People and their pets have special relationships. Many kinds of animals **01**____________(raise) at home by people. These animals **02**____________(dress) in colorful clothes, and expensive food **03**____________(buy) for them to eat. However, pets also help people in many ways. For instance, pets **04**____________(cheer) up people who are sick or living alone. People and their homes **05**____________(protect) by large dogs. In addition, blind people **06**____________(guide) by seeing-eye dogs. These dogs **07**____________(train) to stop walking if they sense a dangerous situation. They also **08**____________(avoid) low branches and other obstacles.

[1-2] 다음 빈칸에 들어가기에 알맞은 것은?

1

> The electric light bulb _______ by Thomas Edison.

① invents ② is inventing
③ invented ④ was invented
⑤ was inventing

2

> Jenny was made _______ the book club.

① join ② joins ③ joined
④ joining ⑤ to join

3 다음 밑줄 친 부분 중 어법상 어색한 것은?

① The bank robber was caught by the police.
② He was made to play the guitar for us.
③ The letter was returned to me last week.
④ She was heard sing a song.
⑤ The boys were seen to play soccer.

4 다음 문장을 수동태로 알맞게 바꾼 것은?

> Jean sent me a letter from the U.S.

① Jean was sent a letter to me from the U.S.
② I was sent Jean a letter from the U.S.
③ I was sent a letter to Jean from the U.S.
④ A letter was sent by Jean me from the U.S.
⑤ A letter was sent to me by Jean from the U.S.

5 다음 중 어법상 어색한 문장은?

① Dragons are called *ryu* in China.
② This airplane is not flying by male pilots.
③ An island is surrounded by water.
④ A wristwatch is worn around the wrist.
⑤ The large class was divided into two parts.

[6-7] 다음 밑줄 친 부분 중 어법상 어색한 것은?

6 My brother was offered a job at a college, ① ② but he didn't accept it. Instead, he was hiring ③ ④ ⑤ at a school.

7 I lost my watch yesterday. I thought it ① ② was stolen at the park, but it found at home ③ ④ ⑤ today.

[8-9] 다음 문장을 수동태로 바꾸어 쓰시오.

8 People speak English in many countries.

→ _______________________________

9 Our teacher bought us some ice cream.

→ _______________________________

10 주어진 단어들을 바르게 배열하시오.

(seen / his friends / were / toward the beach / to head)

→ _______________________________

A: What **is being talked** about in the news?

B : The new Olympic stadium **will be completed** next month!

15 주의해야 할 수동태

수동태의 형태

조동사 + 수동태	조동사 + be + p.p.	The roof **can be fixed** by Kevin. 그 지붕은 Kevin에 의해 고쳐질 수 있다.
	조동사 + have + been p.p. (조동사의 과거)	The song **should have been sung** by me. 그 노래는 나에 의해서 불러져야 했다.
진행형 수동태	be동사 + being p.p.	The hotel **is being built** by the new company. 그 호텔은 새로운 회사에 의해 건축되고 있다.
완료시제 수동태	have/has/had + been p.p.	The problem **has been discussed** for a month. 그 문제는 한 달 동안 논의되어 오고 있다.

e.g. Pets **cannot be allowed** in this restaurant. 이 식당에 애완동물은 들어올 수 없습니다.

The next Olympic Games **will be held** in Korea. 다음 올림픽 게임은 한국에서 열릴 것입니다.

The living room **was being cleaned** when I came. 내가 왔을 때 거실은 청소 중이었다.

수동태로 쓰지 않는 동사

기본적으로 타동사만 수동태로 쓸 수 있으며, 수동태가 되었을 때 의미가 어색해지는 타동사나 수동적인 의미가 포함된 자동사는 수동태로 쓰지 않습니다.

| 타동사 | fit, have, lack, resemble, hold, suit 등
The jeans **don't fit** you. 그 청바지는 너에게 맞지 않아. → You **are not fitted** by the jeans. (x) |
| 자동사 | sell(팔리다), wash(씻겨나가다), taste(~한 맛이 나다), lock(잠기다) 등
These shoes **sell** very well among teenagers. 이 신발은 10대들 사이에서 매우 잘 팔린다.
→ These shoes **are sold** very well among teenagers. (x) |

e.g. I **don't resemble** my mother. 나는 우리 어머니를 닮지 않았다.

This door **locks** behind you automatically. 이 문은 당신이 들어가면 자동으로 잠깁니다.

Fruit stains **don't wash** out well. 과일 얼룩은 잘 씻기지 않는다.

Check up 1

A   괄호 안에서 알맞은 것을 고르시오.

01 The report is (being prepared, been prepared) by Mr. Lee.

02 A new idea can (being suggested, be suggested) by anyone.

03 The room (had not been cleaned, had been not cleaned) then.

04 This olive oil might (have been imported, been have imported) from Greece.

05 The ceiling of the church (has been painting, has been painted) by a famous painter.

06 The whiteboard should (be erased, have erased) after every class.

07 My purse must (have been stolen, have stolen) in the subway.

08 I was (being interviewed, being interviewing) by the manager when you called me.

09 Is a new smart phone (being developed, is developed) by the company?

10 Ann must (have been calling, have been called) to the meeting.

B   다음 밑줄 친 부분을 바르게 고치시오. 맞으면 O로 표시하시오.

01 The big tree was died because of lack of water.   → _______________

02 The travel book sells very well in the market.   → _______________

03 I think James is had the funniest comic book ever.   → _______________

04 The sand washed away from the beach.   → _______________

05 These jeans are suited you well.   → _______________

06 My niece is resembled by my mother.   → _______________

07 I guess something bad will be happened tomorrow. → _______________

08 Is the snack tasted sweet?   → _______________

09 A lot of water is lacking in Africa.   → _______________

10 The door locked improperly, so I couldn't open it.   → _______________

Check up 2

A 다음 가족들의 문제나 고민을 나타낸 표를 보고 문장을 완성하시오.

Problem	Solution	Result
broken washing machine	send it to a service center	the center cannot fix it
dirty backyard	clean it together	clean it this Sunday and plant some new flowers
too old dog house	build a new dog house	father can build a dog house

01 The washing machine might have ______________ because of my mistake.

02 The washing machine ______________ to a service center.

03 The machine ______________ in the center.

04 The dirty backyard ______________ by all of my family members.

05 The backyard will ______________ this Sunday, and new flowers will

______________.

06 A new dog house for our dog ______________ by my father.

B 주어진 단어들을 사용해 글을 완성하시오.

You might know about the Taj Mahal because the story of it **01**______________ (has, tell) by many people so far. The Taj Mahal **02**______________ (has, describe) as the most beautiful building in the world. It **03**______________(locate) in Agra, India, and it **04**______________ (build) three hundred years ago. But no one is sure who designed it. It **05**______________(must, have, design) by many Turkish architects, and generally, Lahauri **06**______________(consider) to have been the head architect. When the tomb **07**______________(being, built), about 20,000 workers and 20 years **08**______________(had, use) to complete it.

Actual Test

[1-2] 다음 빈칸에 들어가기에 알맞은 것은?

1

A new player for the team __________.

① should find
② should have found
③ should be found
④ should be finding
⑤ should have been finding

2

I heard a terrible thing __________ to him.

① happened
② is happened
③ is being happened
④ has been happened
⑤ been happened

3 주어진 문장과 의미가 같은 것은?

Someone had already borrowed the book.

① The book had already been borrowed.
② The book has already been borrowed.
③ The book had already being borrowed.
④ Someone had already been borrowed the book.
⑤ Someone has already been borrowed the book.

4 다음 밑줄 친 부분을 알맞게 고친 것은?

The boy should have punished for telling a lie.

① should punished
② should been punished
③ should been have punished
④ should have being punished
⑤ should have been punished

5 다음 중 어법상 어색한 것은?

① Jeans have been mostly worn by teenagers.
② The laundry must have been doing by dad.
③ I don't resemble any member of my family.
④ Those waffles sell very well.
⑤ A new island will be discovered soon.

[6-7] 다음 밑줄 친 부분 중 어법상 어색한 것은?

6 My chores should have been finished an
①　　　　　②
hour ago, but the vacuum cleaner has breaking.
③　　　④　　　　　⑤

7 Our new house is being building on the
①　　　②　　　③
hill. The entire valley can be seen from it.
④　　　⑤

[8-9] 주어진 말을 바르게 배열하시오.

8 (in 19th century / have / written / this poem / must / been)

→ _______________________

9 (has / skiing / by / loved / many people / been)

→ _______________________

10 다음 밑줄 친 문장을 바르게 고치시오.

10 years ago, people bought groceries at small stores. However, many huge stores have been built. The goods at these big supermarkets are sold well, but their prices are more expensive than those at the small stores.

→ _______________________

Review Test

[1-3] 다음 빈칸에 들어가기에 알맞은 것은?

01

> The picture of me ________ by Jack.

① take   ② takes   ③ taken
④ was take   ⑤ was taken

02

> The dog was ________ at the thief by me.

① seen bark   ② seen to bark
③ seeing bark   ④ seeing to bark
⑤ saw barking

03

> The story should ______ to the other people.

① have told   ② have been telling
③ had told   ④ have been told
⑤ had been telling

[4-5] 다음 빈칸에 들어갈 수 없는 것을 고르시오.

04

> The computer ___________ by me.

① was bought   ② will be used
③ can be upgraded   ④ is suited
⑤ could have been broken

05

> I ___________ by my mom.

① was resembled   ② was punished
③ was washed   ④ was given food
⑤ was made to stay home

[6-7] 빈칸에 들어갈 말이 알맞게 짝지어진 것을 고르시오.

06

> • The boy was heard _(A)_ a beautiful song.
> • This pen can _(B)_ well in the market.

① to sing – be sold   ② to sing – sell
③ to sing – to sell   ④ sing – sell
⑤ sing – to sell

07

> • Your dog should be _(A)_ less.
> • I was made _(B)_ the question.

① feed – to answer   ② fed – answering
③ feed – answering   ④ fed – answer
⑤ fed – to answer

[8-10] 다음 밑줄 친 부분이 어색한 것을 고르시오.

08

① This coat <u>was made</u> in England.
② The stadium <u>will be completed</u> next week.
③ An accident <u>was happened</u> in the street.
④ The cup <u>was dropped</u> by my brother.
⑤ The fire <u>was caused</u> by a cigarette.

09

① The coffee <u>was being made</u> in the room.
② I <u>could have been accepted</u> to the college.
③ The result <u>will be announced</u> today.
④ The picture <u>might have been drawn</u> by her.
⑤ The phone <u>was not finding</u> in the box.

10

① Was the concert <u>being performed</u> at that time?

② The game <u>can be not played</u> by four people.

③ That hat <u>had been made</u> in Mexico.

④ A test <u>will be given</u> to students tomorrow.

⑤ Only the main course <u>has been served</u> so far.

[11-12] 다음 빈칸에 들어가기에 알맞은 것을 고르시오.

11

> The car door _______ automatically.

① is locked   ② locks

③ was locking   ④ was locked

⑤ locking

12

> A serious mistake _______ by her.

① makes   ② is making

③ has made   ④ has been making

⑤ has been made

13 다음 문장을 수동태로 잘못 바꾼 것은?

① They were playing the violins.
→ The violins were being played by them.

② They gave Ann many presents for her birthday.
→ Many presents were given to Ann for her birthday.

③ I think him a real leader.
→ A real leader was thought him by me.

④ I will take care of his pet during his trip.
→ His pet will be taken care of by me during his trip.

⑤ My mother heard me call him.
→ I was heard to call him by my mother.

[14-15] 두 문장의 뜻이 일치하도록 빈칸에 알맞은 말을 고르시오.

14

> The company paid Sarah much money.
>
> = Sarah _____ much money by the company.

① pay   ② paid   ③ was paid

④ was paying   ⑤ being paid

15

> Jay asked his teacher a hard question.
>
> = His teacher _____________.

① asked Jay a hard question

② was asked Jay a hard question

③ was asking a hard question by Jay

④ was asked a hard question by Jay

⑤ been asked a hard question by Jay

[16-18] 주어진 우리말을 영어로 알맞게 옮긴 것을 고르시오.

16

> Peter는 카페에서 메뉴를 건네 받았다.

① Peter handed a menu at the café.

② Peter is handing a menu at the café.

③ Peter had handed a menu at the café.

④ Peter was handing a menu at the café.

⑤ Peter was handed a menu at the café.

17

청구서는 이번 달에 전송될 것입니다.

① The bill will have been sent this month.
② The bill will send this month.
③ The bill will be sending this month.
④ The bill will be sent this month.
⑤ The bill will have sent this month.

18

학교에서 점심이 무료로 제공될 수 있습니까?

① Can be lunch served for free at school?
② Can be lunch serving for free at school?
③ Can lunch be served for free at school?
④ Can lunch be serving for free at school?
⑤ Can lunch be been served for free at school?

[19-21] 다음 문장을 수동태로 바꿀 때 빈칸에 알맞은 말을 쓰시오.

19

The adventurers had discovered the old temple.

→ The old temple ___________________ by the adventurers.

20

Is our soccer team winning the game?

→ Is ______________ by our soccer team?

21

The dog can guide blind people.

→ Blind people ______________ by the dog.

[22-23] 어법상 어색한 부분을 찾아 바르게 고치시오.

22

___________ → ___________

More than 50 kinds of fish had been found in the lake. Some of the fish were newly naming by scientists.

23

___________ → ___________

I spent almost a month sitting in front of a computer. Many games had been playing with the computer.

[24-25] 다음 글을 읽고 물음에 답하시오.

One sunny afternoon, while his brothers and sisters were playing, Martin stayed in his room. He ①was buried in a book about planets and stars. The ceiling and walls of Martin's bedroom ②were covered with stars. Martin ③made sure the stars ④were placed in their right positions. For the school science fair, weeks ⑤were spending building a model of the solar system by Martin. (A) The model picked for the first prize by his teacher.

24 위 글의 밑줄 친 부분 중 어법상 어색한 것은?

①　　　②　　　③　　　④　　　⑤

25 위 글의 (A)를 바르게 고쳐 쓰시오.

→ ___________________________

Appendix

01 동사의 3단 변화

틀리기 쉬운 규칙 변화

의 미	원 형	과거형	과거분사형
거짓말하다	lie	lied	lied
눕다, 놓여 있다	lie	lay	lain
눕히다, 놓다	lay	laid	laid
앉다	sit	sat	sat
앉히다	seat	seated	seated
발견하다	find	found	found
설립하다	found	founded	founded
부상 입다	wound	wounded	wounded
튀어 오르다	bound	bounded	bounded
오르다, 상승하다	rise	rose	risen
올리다	raise	raised	raised
생기다	arise	arose	arisen

A-B-A

의 미	원 형	과거형	과거분사형
오다	come	came	come
되다	become	became	become
달리다	run	ran	run

A-B-B

의 미	원 형	과거형	과거분사형
구부리다	bend	bent	bent
피가 나다	bleed	bled	bled
데리고 오다	bring	brought	brought
짓다	build	built	built
사다	buy	bought	bought
잡다	catch	caught	caught
파다	dig	dug	dug
먹이를 주다	feed	fed	fed
느끼다	feel	felt	felt
싸우다	fight	fought	fought
찾다	find	found	found
얻다	get	got	got [gotten]
가지다	have	had	had
듣다	hear	heard	heard
붙잡다	hold	held	held
지키다	keep	kept	kept

이끌다	lead	led	led
떠나다	leave	left	left
빌려주다	lend	lent	lent
잃다	lose	lost	lost
만들다	make	made	made
의미하다	mean	meant	meant
만나다	meet	met	met
지불하다	pay	paid	paid
말하다	say	said	said
팔다	sell	sold	sold
보내다	send	sent	sent
빛나다	shine	shone	shone
자다	sleep	slept	slept
쓰다	spend	spent	spent
가르치다	teach	taught	taught
말하다	tell	told	told
생각하다	think	thought	thought

A-B-C

의 미	원 형	과거형	과거분사형
낳다	bear	bore	born
시작하다	begin	began	begun
씹다	bite	bit	bitten
불다	blow	blew	blown
깨다	break	broke	broken
선택하다	choose	chose	chosen
하다	do	did	done
당기다	draw	drew	drawn
마시다	drink	drank	drunk
운전하다	drive	drove	driven
먹다	eat	ate	eaten
떨어지다	fall	fell	fallen
날다	fly	flew	flown
잊다	forget	forgot	forgotten
얼다	freeze	froze	frozen
주다	give	gave	given
가다	go	went	gone
자라다	grow	grew	grown
숨기다	hide	hid	hidden
알다	know	knew	known
타다	ride	rode	ridden
흔들다	shake	shook	shaken
보여주다	show	showed	shown

노래 부르다	sing	sang	sung
가라앉다	sink	sank	sunk
말하다	speak	spoke	spoken
훔치다	steal	stole	stolen
헤엄치다	swim	swam	swum
가지다	take	took	taken
찢다	tear	tore	torn
던지다	throw	threw	thrown
깨우다	wake	woke	waken
입다	wear	wore	worn
쓰다	write	wrote	written

A-A-A

의 미	원 형	과거형	과거분사형
터지다	burst	burst	burst
던지다	cast	cast	cast
비용이 들다	cost	cost	cost
자르다	cut	cut	cut
때리다	hit	hit	hit
다치다	hurt	hurt	hurt
시키다	let	let	let
두다	put	put	put
읽다	read	read	read
놓다	set	set	set
닫다	shut	shut	shut
쪼개다	split	split	split
퍼지다	spread	spread	spread

02 형용사의 형태 변화

규칙 변화

의 미	원 형	비교급	최상급
빠른	fast	faster	fastest
키가 큰	tall	taller	tallest
작은	small	smaller	smallest
긴	long	longer	longest
짧은	short	shorter	shortest
젊은	young	younger	youngest
나이든	old	older/elder	oldest/eldest
새로운	new	newer	newest

단자음 + 단모음

의 미	원 형	비교급	최상급
큰	big	bigger	biggest
더운	hot	hotter	hottest
뚱뚱한	fat	fatter	fattest
날씬한	thin	thinner	thinnest

-y로 끝나는 단어

의 미	원 형	비교급	최상급
예쁜	pretty	prettier	prettiest
행복한	happy	happier	happiest
일찍	early	earlier	earliest
바쁜	busy	busier	busiest

3음절 이상 / -ly, -ous, -ful, -ive로 끝나는 단어

의 미	원 형	비교급	최상급
유명한	famous	more famous	most famous
유용한	useful	more useful	most useful
중요한	important	more important	most important
값비싼	expensive	more expensive	most expensive
재미있는	interesting	more interesting	most interesting

불규칙 변화

의 미	원 형	비교급	최상급
좋은/좋게	good/well	better	best
나쁜/해로운	bad/ill	worse	worst
많은	many/much	more	most
적은	little	less	least

03 혼동되는 어휘 모음

어휘	품사/의미	어휘	품사/의미
hard	(형) 딱딱한 (부) 열심히	lonely	(형) 외로운
hardly	(부) 거의 ~하지 않다	alone	(부) 혼자
late	(형) 늦은 (부) 늦게	high	(형) 높은 (부) 높게
lately	(부) 최근에	highly	(부) 매우
later	(부) 나중에	near	(전) ~ 가까이에
latter	(형) 후자의	nearly	(부) 거의
most	(형) 가장 ~ 한	close	(동) 닫다 (형) 가까운
mostly	(부) 주로, 일반적으로	closely	(부) 자세히, 면밀히

Memo
Memo

까칠한

감성 맞춤 내신 공략

Grammar

길들이기

내신 만점을 향한 중등 영어 문법 기본서

- 최신 개정 교육과정 분석 및 반영
- 내신에서 꼭 출제되는 핵심 문법만 쉽고 간단하게!
- 효과적인 1일 학습량 제시:
- 〈개념 이해〉→〈기본〉→〈응용〉→〈실전문제〉의 체계적인 4단계 구성
- 통합 서술형 문제를 비롯한 최신 출제 경향 반영

마무리 1

까칠한 Grammar 길들이기

감성 맞춤 내신 공략

마무리 1

woongjin compass

명사와 대명사

UNIT 01 | 명사의 종류
p.08

해석 나는 아침에 한잔의 우유를 마신다.
나는 또 삶은 달걀 몇 개를 먹는다.
그것들은 모두 Kevin 삼촌의 농장에서 나온 것이다.

Check up 1
p.09

A 01 an umbrella 02 computer 03 water
04 wood 05 hours 06 the smoke
07 gold 08 bread 09 dollars 10 the salt

B 01 the, United States 02 Sunday
03 China 04 Ms. Smith 05 The, White
House 06 Seoul 07 the, Pacific Ocean
08 The, *New York Times* 09 Mt. Everest
10 Europe

A

01 엄마는 아침에 나에게 우산을 주셨다.

02 Jerry는 새 컴퓨터를 원한다.

03 찬 물이 좀 있나요?

04 우리는 탁자를 만들기 위해서 목재가 필요하다.

05 나는 숙제를 끝내는 데 두 시간이 필요하다.

06 그 연기는 어디에서 나오는 거니?

07 이 귀고리는 금으로 된 것이다.

08 빵과 우유가 조금 남아있다.

09 그 새 펜은 2달러이다.

10 테이블 위에 있는 소금을 건네주세요.

해설 01 가산명사, 단수 02 가산명사, 단수 03 불가산명사 04 불가산명사 05 가산명사, 복수 06 불가산명사 07 불가산명사 08 불가산명사 09 가산명사, 복수 10 불가산명사

B

01 Tom은 미국에 산다.

02 오늘은 일요일이다.

03 나는 중국에 가고 싶다.

04 너는 Ms. Smith를 아니?

05 백악관은 미국의 대통령이 사는 곳이다.

06 서울은 우리 나라의 수도이다.

07 이 지구본에서 태평양은 어디에 있니?

08 뉴욕타임즈는 신문 회사이다.

09 Ted는 이번 겨울에 에베레스트 산을 오를 계획이다.

10 너는 유럽에 가본 적이 있니?

해설 01 부정관사 the 02 관사 X 03 관사 X 04 관사 X 05 부정관사 the 06 관사 X 07 부정관사 the 08 부정관사 the 09 관사 X 10 관사 X

Check up 2
p.10

A 01 advice 02 beauty 03 hope
04 weather 05 art

B 01 Sunday 02 Janice 03 books
04 Japan 05 milk 06 bread
07 information 08 juice 09 time

A

01 할머니는 나에게 좋은 조언을 해 주신다.

02 Sarah는 아름답기로 유명하다.

03 나는 내 지갑을 찾을 희망이 하나도 없다.

04 대부분의 사람들은 비 내리는 날씨를 싫어한다.

05 미술관에는 유명한 예술 작품들이 있다.

B

나는 지난 일요일에 쇼핑을 하러 갔다. 백화점에 가는 길에 나는 Janice를 만났다. 그녀는 일본에 대한 책을 사고 싶어 했다. 왜냐하면 그곳에 갈 계획이었기 때문이다. 나도 우유 두 병과 빵을 사야 했다. 그래서 우리는 가게에 함께 갔다. 그녀는 많은 여행 정보가 들어 있는 책을 샀다. 쇼핑을 한 후에 우리는 주스를 마시고 집으로 돌아왔다. 나는 그녀와 즐거운 시간을 보냈다.

해설 01 고유명사 02 고유명사 03 가산명사, 복수형 04 고유명사 05 불가산명사 06 불가산명사 07 불가산명사 08 불가산명사 09 불가산명사

Actual Test   p.11

1 ③   2 ⑤   3 ③   4 ③   5 ①   6 ④   7 ⑤
8 ③ → the Han River   9 ④ → water
10 You can see a lion and two tigers here.

---

1 meter는 가산명사이며 빈칸에는 복수형이 들어간다.

2 air는 불가산명사이므로 a(n)와 함께 쓰일 수 없다.

3 advice는 불가산명사로 복수형이 될 수 없다.

4 butter는 불가산명사로 복수형이 될 수 없다.

5 고유명사 Pacific Ocean 앞에는 the를 쓰며, daughter는 가산명사 단수형이므로 앞에 a가 들어간다.

6 고유명사 London앞에는 the를 붙이지 않는다.

7 dollar는 가산명사이므로 복수형 dollars가 되어야 한다.

8 고유명사 Han River 앞에는 the를 붙인다.

9 water는 불가산명사이므로 복수형이 될 수 없다.

10 lion은 가산명사로 단수로 쓰일 경우 앞에 꼭 부정관사 a나 the를 붙인다.

UNIT 02 | 대명사   p.12

해석 A: 저것들은 뭐니?

B: 저것들은 내 책이야. 갖고 싶은 거 있니?

A: 응. 그 책들 중에서 읽고 싶은 게 조금 있어.

Check up 1   p.13

A 01 himself   02 itself   03 he   04 her
05 herself   06 Mine   07 ourselves   08 His
09 him   10 us

B 01 these   02 That   03 one   04 That
05 Some   06 others   07 the others
08 one   09 the other   10 the other

A

01 혼자 있을 때 Jason은 혼잣말을 한다.

02 그 음식 자체는 맛있지 않았다.

03 Paul은 그가 정말 싫어했던 직장을 관두었다.

04 그 강한 햇빛은 그녀의 눈을 상하게 했다.

05 우리 언니는 강가에 혼자서 산다.

06 네 우산을 같이 써도 될까? 내 것은 너무 작아.

07 내 친구와 나는 우리들의 사진을 찍었다.

08 그의 친구가 더 좋은 생각을 떠올렸다.

09 매니저는 어제 그에게 돈을 주었다.

10 선생님은 수업을 일찍 끝내시겠다고 우리에게 약속했다.

> **해설** 01 재귀대명사 02 재귀대명사 03 주격 / 3인칭 남자 단수 04 소유격 05 재귀대명사. by oneself : 혼자서 06 소유대명사 07 1인칭 복수 08 소유격 09 목적격 10 목적격

B

01 이리 와서 쿠키를 좀 먹으럼. 이것들은 내가 만든 거야.

02 저기 멀리 서 있는 저 여자는 누구니? – 저건 내 사촌이야.

03 고양이에 대한 책이 좀 있니? 하나 읽고 싶어.

04 Beth는 나에 대한 안 좋은 이야기를 했어. 그게 날 정말 화나게 했어.

05 그 관광객 중 몇몇은 일본에서 왔다.

06 어떤 여자아이들은 집 안에서 노는 것을 좋아하지만 다른 여자아이들은 그렇지 않다.

07 나에겐 형이 세 명 있다. 한 명은 나보다 크고, 나머지는 나보다 작다.

08 빨간 펜이 있니? – 응, 하나 있어.

09 Jenny는 사촌이 두 명 있다. 한 명은 도시에 살고, 다른 한 명은 농장에 산다.

10 그 가게는 두 종류의 과일을 판다. 하나는 멜론이고 나머지는 체리이다.

> **해설** 01 복수 02 멀리 떨어진 사람 03 a book about cat을 대신하는 부정대명사 04 문장 전체는 단수 취급 05 불특정한 일부를 나타내는 some 06 또 다른 일부를 나타내는 others 07 정해진 수 중 마지막 남은 여럿 08 a red pen을 대신하는 부정대명사 09 둘 중 나머지 하나 10 둘 중 나머지 하나

Check up 2

A 01 His 02 me 03 any 04 others
   05 him 06 It 07 the others 08 other
B 01 they 02 them 03 my 04 They
   05 themselves 06 these 07 It 08 Its
   09 myself 10 That

A

01 Jerry는 내 가장 친한 친구이다. 그의 생일은 2월 28일이다.

02 내 생일은 8월이어서 Jerry가 나보다 한 살 더 많다.

03 Jerry에게는 형제들이 있지만 나는 아무도 없다.

04 Jerry는 형제가 세 명 있다. 한 명은 나보다 나이가 많고, 나머지는 나보다 어리다.

05 Jerry는 거의 매일 기타를 친다. 그건 그를 행복하게 한다.

06 나는 요가 하는 것을 좋아한다. 그건 내 건강에 좋다.

07 Jerry의 가족은 다섯 명이다. 두 명은 부모님이며, 나머지는 모두 그의 형제들이다.

08 나는 애완견 두 마리가 있다. 하나는 흰색이고, 다른 하나는 검정색이다.

해설 01 소유격 02 목적격 03 부정문에서는 any사용 04 나머지 둘 05 목적격 06 yoga를 it으로 받음 07 나머지 하나 08 둘 중 나머지 하나

B

펭귄은 재미있는 동물이다. 나는 그들이 매우 귀엽다고 생각해서 내 과학 과제로 골랐다. 그들은 새이지만 스스로 날 수 없다. 수백만 년 전에 그들에게는 날개가 있었다. 하지만 이 날개들은 쓸모가 없어졌는데, 그들은 그다지 날 필요가 없었기 때문이다. 펭귄은 물고기를 먹는다. 그것은 물에 살기 때문에 날개는 지느러미가 되었다. 펭귄의 나는 능력은 더 이상 필요치 않았다. 혼자 동물원에 가면 나는 항상 펭귄을 보며 시간을 보낸다. 그건 매번 나를 미소 짓게 한다.

해설 01 Penguins 지칭 02 목적격 03 소유격 04 penguins 지칭 05 재귀대명사 06 wings (복수) 지칭 07 The penguin 지칭 08 소유격 09 재귀대명사 10 문장 전체 지칭

Actual Test

1 ③ 2 ④ 3 ② 4 ⑤ 5 ④ 6 ⑤ 7 ④
8 She is looking at herself
9 These are my favorite doughnuts.
10 That is Sarah

1 ③은 소유대명사이며, 나머지는 모두 소유격이다.

2 we의 재귀대명사가 들어가야 한다. by oneself는 '혼자서' 라는 의미이다.

3 (A)에는 목적격, (B)에는 소유격이 들어가야 한다.

4 문장에서 you가 복수로 쓰였으므로 ⑤는 yourselves가 되어야 한다.

5 둘 중 나머지 하나는 the other로 나타낸다.

6 others는 복수이므로 ⑤번에는 are가 들어가며, 나머지는 모두 is가 들어간다.

7 세 나라 중 마지막이므로 The other가 되어야 한다.

8 자기 자신을 보고 있으므로 재귀대명사 herself를 쓴다.

9 가까이 있는 복수명사는 these를 쓴다.

10 멀리 있는 사람이나 사물은 that으로 표현한다.

Review Test

01 ④ 02 ⑤ 03 ④ 04 ③ 05 ① 06 ⑤
07 ④ 08 ⑤ 09 ② 10 ① 11 ⑤ 12 ②
13 ⑤ 14 ② 15 ③ 16 ⑤ 17 gave me a cup of milk 18 One is red and the other
19 ⑤ 20 ④ 21 others → the others 22 one → ones 23 ① 24 (A) They (B) it

01 목적격 – 소유대명사의 관계이다.

02 목적격 – 재귀대명사의 관계이다.

03 friend와 나머지 명사들은 가산명사이나, advice는 불가산명사이다.

04 information은 추상명사이나, building은 추상명사가 아니라 보통명사이다.

05 juice와 나머지 명사들은 불가산명사이나 meter는 가산명사이다.

06 뒤에 명사가 온 것으로 보아, 빈칸에는 소유격이 들어가야 하나 us는 목적격이다.

07 앞에 동사가 온 것으로 보아, 빈칸에는 목적격이 들어가야 하나 yours는 소유대명사이다.

08 cup은 가산명사이므로 앞에 관사를 써야 한다.

09 The United States(미국)는 단수 취급한다.

10 ② hour → hours, ③ breads → bread, ④ A → x, ⑤ a → the

11 some은 불특정한 일부, other는 다른 일부를 가리킨다.

12 White House와 United States 앞에는 the를 붙인다.

13 빈칸에는 we의 소유대명사 ourselves가 들어간다. by oneself는 '혼자서'의 의미이다.

14 멀리 떨어진 사물을 가리킬 때는 지시대명사 that을 쓴다.

15 advice는 불가산명사이고 나머지는 모두 가산명사이다.

16 ⑤의 hers는 소유대명사이며, 나머지는 소유격이다.

17 milk는 물질명사로 a cup of를 써서 센다.

18 정해진 둘 중 하나는 one, 나머지 하나는 the other를 써서 나타낸다.

19 happiness는 셀 수 없는 추상명사이다.

20 book의 재귀대명사는 itself이다.

21 남은 책이 복수(두 권)이므로 others가 아닌 the others가 들어가야 한다.

22 shoes는 복수이므로 one이 아닌 ones가 되어야 한다.

23 the United States(미국)은 복수형으로 쓴다.

24 (A)에는 3인칭 복수인 Two different games를 가리키는 they가 들어가야 하며, (B)에는 the ball을 가리키는 it이 들어가야 한다.

UNIT 03 | 단순시제   p.20

해석 어제는 비가 많이 왔다.

이 지역에는 보통 여름에 비가 많이 온다.

이번 주말에 또 비가 올 것이다.

● Check up 1   p.21

A 01 washes 02 went 03 travels
04 leaves 05 visited 06 begins 07 left
08 wakes 09 will go 10 goes

B 01 o 02 returns → returned 03 will be
→ was 04 o 05 lose → lost 06 o
07 laughed → laughs 08 o 09 o
10 flowed → flows

A

01 Diane은 이틀에 한 번씩 머리를 감는다.

02 우리 아버지는 20년 전에 대학에 다니셨다.

03 나는 빛이 소리보다 더 빨리 움직인다고 들었다.

04 서울로 가는 기차는 10분 뒤에 떠난다.

05 그의 친구들 중 몇몇이 지난 주말에 그를 방문했다.

06 공연은 매주 일요일 8시 30분에 시작한다.

07 그 기차는 5분 전에 역을 떠났어요.

08 아침에, 내 창문의 태양이 나를 깨운다.

09 나는 책을 못 찾아서, 내일 서점에 다시 갈 것이다.

10 우리는 John이 떠날 때 그를 위해 파티를 열 것이다.

> **해설** 01 현재: 평소 습관 02 과거: twenty years ago
> 03 현재: 불변의 진리 04 현재: 왕래발착동사 05 과
> 거: last weekend 06 현재: 반복되는 일 07 과거:
> five minutes ago 08 현재: 반복되는 일
> 09 미래: tomorrow 10 현재: 시간의 부사절에서 현재
> 가 미래를 대신

B

01 나는 아침에 항상 아침을 먹는다.

02 Jack은 어제 그 책을 반납했다.

03 Alice는 창문이 깨졌을 때 교실에 있었다.

04 비행기는 30분 뒤에 출발합니다.

05 나는 지난 금요일에 도서관에서 사전을 잃어버렸다.

06 옷은 햇볕 아래에서 잘 마른다.

07 그녀는 텔레비전을 볼 때 보통 많이 웃는다.

08 내가 어제 들었던 노래는 전혀 좋지 않았다.

09 우리는 오늘 밤 네가 오기 전에 저녁 준비를 마칠 거야.

10 물은 높은 곳에서 낮은 곳으로 흐른다.

> **해설** 02 과거: yesterday 03 과거: 종속절(과거)
> 05 과거: last Friday 07 현재: 평소의 습관 10 현재:
> 불변의 진리

● Check up 2   p.22

A 01 bought some books 02 studied
English 03 went shopping 04 met
05 goes 06 will write[am going to write]
07 will stay[am going to stay] 08 will go
[is going to go]

B 01 rained 02 is 03 will rain 04 is
05 seems 06 snowed 07 will snow
08 escaped

A

01 나는 지난 월요일에 책을 몇 권 샀다.

02 Carrie는 어제 친구들과 영어 공부를 했다.

03 나는 어제 쇼핑을 했다.

04 나는 화요일에 상점에서 친구들 몇몇을 만났다.

05 Carrie는 주중에는 보통 수영을 한다.

06 나는 내일 에세이를 쓸 것이다.

07 나는 이번 주말에 집에 있을 것이다.

08 Carrie는 이번 주말에 캠핑을 갈 것이다.

> **해설** 01 과거: last Monday 02 과거: yesterday
> 03 과거: yesterday 04 과거: 지난 화요일의 일
> 05 현재: 습관, 반복되는 일 06 미래: tomorrow
> 07 미래: 다가올 주말 08 미래: 다가올 주말

B

앵커: 좋은 아침입니다. 오늘의 날씨는 어떤가요?

예보관: 창문 밖을 보십시오. 어제 비가 왔다는 게 믿겨지나요? 지금 여러분은 매우 화창한 것을 볼 수 있을 것입니다. 하지만 오후에는 또다시 비가 많이 내리겠습니다. 이 계절에는 비가 거의 내리지 않는 게 보통입니다. 요즘에는 많은 사람들이 생각하는 것처럼 날씨가 이상한 것 같습니다.

앵커: 그렇군요. 전 세계 다른 나라들의 날씨는 어떤가요?

예보관: 음, 호주에서는 어제 눈이 많이 내렸습니다. 그리고 내일도 눈이 내릴 것입니다. 또 동아시아 해변에 있는 많은 사람들은 지난 밤에 강력한 태풍으로부터 대피했습니다.

> **해설** **01** 과거: yesterday **02** 현재: now **03** 미래: 다가올 오후 **04** 현재: 평소의 습관 **05** 현재: 평소의 상태 **06** 과거: yesterday **07** 미래: tomorrow **08** 과거: last night

Actual Test
p.23

1 ③ **2** ④ **3** ② **4** ⑤ **5** ③ **6** ④ **7** ②

8 Jack doesn't write a report for homework.

9 The scientists did research about weather.

10 we bought some healthy snacks in the grocery store

1 usually로 보아, 평소의 습관을 나타내므로 현재시제가 쓰인다.

2 last weekend는 '지난 주말'로 과거를 나타내므로 pick은 과거형 picked가 되어야 한다.

3 ②는 과거시제이나, 나머지는 모두 현재시제이다.

4 (A)에는 later로 보아 미래시제, (B)에는 yesterday가 있으므로, 과거시제, (C)는 불변의 진리에 해당하므로 현재시제로 쓴다.

5 last Saturday는 '지난 토요일'로 과거를 나타내므로 watched가 되어야 한다.

6 in the future는 미래를 나타내므로 will continue가 되어야 한다.

7 다가올 주말, 즉 미래의 계획을 묻고 있다.

8 현재시제에서 일반동사의 3인칭 단수 부정형은 does not을 쓴다.

9 do의 과거형은 did이다.

10 「주어 + 동사 + 목적어 + 부사구」 순으로 나열한다. 이미 일어난 일에 대한 것은 과거시제로 쓴다.

UNIT 04 | 완료시제
p.24

해석 나는 이미 점심을 먹었어.

나는 어머니가 도착했을 때, 한 시간째 집에 있는 중이었다.

나는 다음 일요일까지는 일을 끝마쳤을 것이다.

Check up 1

p.25

A **01** seen **02** had **03** drawn **04** has **05** will have **06** slept **07** ridden **08** had **09** have **10** will have

B **01** have never eaten **02** has known **03** has not taken **04** will have started **05** had been **06** has never seen **07** had already closed **08** had just given **09** has not had **10** has won

A

01 나는 하늘에서 별똥별을 한번도 본 적이 없다.

02 James는 나에게 자동차 사고가 났었다고 말했다.

03 자화상을 그려본 적이 있니?

04 나는 그 남자가 바이올린을 한번도 켜본 적이 없다고 생각해.

05 그는 내년이면 5년째 바그다드에 사는 것이 된다.

06 우리 엄마는 텐트 안에서 자본 적이 없다.

07 너는 전에 말을 타본 적이 있니?

08 나는 Lisa가 전에 시험에서 부정행위를 했다고 확신했다.

09 그들은 2001년부터 이 집에 살아왔다.

10 그녀는 다음 주면 3개월 동안 이곳에서 일한 거야.

> **해설** **01** 현재완료: 경험 **02** 과거완료 **03** 현재완료: 경험 **04** 현재완료: 경험 **05** 미래완료 **06** 현재완료: 경험 **07** 현재완료: 경험 **08** 과거완료 **09** 미래완료 **10** 미래완료

B

01 나는 지금까지 바닷가재를 먹어본 적이 없다.

02 Tina는 Sarah를 10년째 알고 지낸다.

03 그는 자신의 낡은 카메라를 잃어버린 이후로 사진을 찍은 적이 없었다.

04 연주회는 그가 여기 도착할 때쯤에는 시작했을 것이다.

05 Sam은 요리사가 되기 전에는 사업가였다.

06 그 소녀는 전에 눈을 본 적이 한번도 없다.

07 동물원은 내가 도착했을 때 이미 닫았었다.

08 교실에 도착했을 때 선생님은 퀴즈를 낸 상태였다.

09 그녀는 지난 학기 이후로 여유 시간이 없었다.

10 복권에 당첨이 된 사람을 알고 있니?

> **해설** **01** 현재완료: 경험 **02** 현재완료: 계속 **03** 현재완료: 계속 **04** 미래완료 **05** 과거완료 **06** 현재완료: 경험 **07** 과거완료 **08** 과거완료 **09** 현재완료: 계속 **10** 현재완료: 경험

Check up 2 — p.26

A **01** had written **02** had gone jogging **03** did[had done] **04** had cooked **05** have had lunch **06** has, seen **07** will have met **08** will have posted

B **01** have you visited **02** have been **03** have never been **04** have traveled **05** had gone **06** have always wanted **07** have not[haven't] had **08** will have left

A

01 나는 Jenny's에서 점심을 먹기 전에 독후감을 썼다.

02 Ann은 내가 독후감을 쓰기 전에 조깅을 했었다.

03 나는 오전 9시 전까지는 아무것도 하지 않았었다.

04 Ann은 치과에 가기 위해 집을 나서기 전에 버거를 요리했었다.

05 지금 나는 Jenny's에서 친구들과 점심을 다 먹었다.

06 Ann은 방금 막 치과에 다녀왔다.

07 Ann은 내가 집에서 저녁을 먹을 때쯤 City Park에서 Sam을 만날 것이다.

08 나는 오늘 밤 10시까지는 내 에세이를 온라인에 올렸을 것이다.

> **해설** **01** 과거완료 **02** 과거완료 **03** 과거 또는 과거완료 **04** 과거완료 **05** 현재완료 **06** 현재완료 **07** 미래완료 **08** 미래완료

B

Jack: 너는 여행을 좋아하니?

Bora: 응. 나는 정말 여행이 좋아.

Jack: 지금까지 어느 나라를 가 봤니?

Bora: 음, 나는 미국, 일본, 그리고 중국에 가 봤어.

Jack: 나는 그 나라 중에 어떤 곳도 가본 적이 없어. 하지만 나는 러시아를 여행한 적이 있어. 그곳에 있었을 때, 나는 모스크바에 갔었지.

Bora: 그거 재미있네! 나는 거기 항상 가보고 싶었는데.

Jack: 그런데 나는 해외 여행을 할 기회가 많지 않았어. 너는 올해에는 해외에 나갈 계획이 있니?

Bora: 응! 나는 여름 방학이 시작할 때 쯤, 이 나라를 떠나 있을 거야!

> **해설** **01** 현재완료: 경험 **02** 현재완료: 경험 **03** 현재완료: 경험 **04** 현재완료: 경험 **05** 과거완료 **06** 현재완료: 계속 **07** 현재완료: 경험 **08** 미래완료

Actual Test — p.27

1 ③ **2** ④ **3** ① **4** ⑤ **5** ② **6** ④ **7** ②

8 He has not[hasn't] found his wallet.

9 Have you enjoyed yourself at the party?

10 has read many novels before

1 현재완료이므로 빈칸에는 teach의 과거분사인 taught이 들어간다.

2 특정 과거 시점 이전(until yesterday)에 일어난 일이므로 과거완료 시제가 되어야 한다.

3 (A)에는 경험을 묻는 현재완료의 has, (B)에는 특정 과거 시점 이전의 일을 나타내는 과거완료의 had가 들어가야 한다.

4 ⑤의 by the time 이하는 미래 시점이므로 미래완료인 「will+have p.p.」의 형태로 쓰여야 한다. 따라서 has는 will have로 바뀌어야 한다.

5 yesterday는 과거 시점을 나타내므로 현재완료와 함께 쓸 수 없다.

6 과거 이전의 일을 나타내므로 ④의 haven't는 hadn't 가 되어 과거완료가 되어야 한다.

7 시간의 부사절에서는 현재가 미래를 대신하므로 has arrived는 arrives가 되어야 한다.

8 현재완료 부정은 「has＋not＋p.p.」이다.

9 현재완료 의문문은 「Have＋주어＋p.p.~?」형태이다.

10 「has＋p.p.＋목적어＋부사」의 순서이다.

UNIT 05 | 진행형 p.28

해석 내가 집에 도착했을 때. 내 동생은 자전거를 타고 있었다. 그 애는 두 시간째 그것을 타고 있었다.

Check up 1 p.29

A **01** is making **02** was cleaning **03** will be taking **04** been painting **05** been falling **06** was playing **07** is pouring **08** will have been waiting **09** had been using **10** has been flying

B **01** is rising **02** weren't reading **03** was **04** has been writing **05** will have been sleeping **06** will be riding **07** has been talking **08** goes **09** had been swimming **10** has been watching

A

01 그녀는 지금 그녀의 아이들을 위해 연을 만들고 있다.

02 내가 들어왔을 때 그 작은 로봇은 방을 청소하고 있었다.

03 Gary는 내일 이때쯤 영어 수업을 듣고 있는 중일 것이다.

04 나는 엄마를 위해 오래된 가구에 페인트 칠을 하고 있던 중이다.

05 거의 하루 내내 비가 내리고 있었다.

06 내가 홀에 들어섰을 때 그 소년은 기타를 치고 있었다.

07 내 남동생은 지금 모두에게 물을 따라주는 중이다.

08 우리는 그것이 문을 열 때쯤 한 시간째 기다리고 있는 중일 것이다.

09 사람들은 1990년대 전에 힘든 일에 로봇을 사용해 오고 있었다.

10 비행기는 태평양 위를 한 시간째 나는 중이다.

> **해설** **01** 현재진행 **02** 과거진행 **03** 미래진행 **04** 현재완료진행 **05** 과거완료진행 **06** 과거진행 **07** 현재진행 **08** 미래완료진행 **09** 과거완료진행 **10** 현재완료진행

B

01 그 로켓은 지금 하늘 위로 날아오르고 있다.

02 너는 내가 들어갔을 때 책을 읽고 있지 않았어.

03 지난밤에 여기서 자동차 사고가 있었다.

04 Jack은 정오부터 계속 기말 에세이를 쓰고 있던 중이었다.

05 내가 집에 갈 때쯤이면 그녀는 10시간째 자고 있을 것이다.

06 나는 다음 주말 이때쯤이면 제주도에서 자전거를 타고 있을 것이다.

07 그는 한 시간째 여자친구와 이야기하고 있는 중이다.

08 Julia는 항상 자정이 되기 전에 잠자리에 든다.

09 네가 전화했을 때 나는 체육관에서 수영을 하고 있던 중이었어.

10 Mary 이모는 오전 내내 다큐멘터리를 보고 계셔.

> **해설** **01** 현재진행 **02** 과거진행 **03** 단순과거 **04** 현재완료진행 **05** 미래완료진행 **06** 미래진행 **07** 현재완료진행 **08** 단순현재 **09** 과거완료진행 **10** 현재완료진행

Check up 2 p.30

A **01** was reading **02** has been reading **03** was drawing **04** was taking **05** is riding **06** are playing **07** have been playing

B **01** don't enjoy **02** had decided **03** had been planning **04** had been watching **05** was **06** have been searching **07** are looking **08** will be walking

A

01 내가 그를 보았을 때 그 노인은 신문을 읽고 있었다.

02 그 노인은 두 시간째 그 신문을 읽고 있다.

03 긴 머리의 여자는 남자가 개와 함께 나왔을 때, 그림을

그리고 있던 중이었다.

04 개를 데리고 있는 그 남자는 두 시간 전에 산책을 하고 있었다.

05 자전거를 타고 있는 남자는 지금 자전거를 매우 천천히 타고 가는 중이다.

06 남자와 여자는 지금 배드민턴을 치고 있다.

07 남자와 여자는 두 시간째 배드민턴을 치고 있는 것 같다.

> **해설** **01** 과거진행 **02** 현재완료진행 **03** 과거진행
> **04** 과거진행 **05** 현재진행 **06** 현재진행 **07** 현재완료
> 진행

B

John과 나는 평소에 여행을 좋아하는 편이 아니지만, 우리는 시도를 해보기로 했다. 우리는 뉴욕에 가기로 계획을 세우던 중이었다. John은 TV에서 영화를 보고 있었고, 거기에는 이탈리아의 아름다운 광경이 있었다. 그때부터 우리는 지금까지 그 나라에 대한 정보를 찾아오고 있는 중이다. 지금 우리는 머무를 호텔을 찾아보고 있다. 우리는 매우 신이 난다. 우리는 다음 달 이때쯤 로마를 걷고 있을 것이다!

> **해설** **01** 단순현재 **02** 과거완료 **03** 과거완료진행
> **04** 과거완료진행 **05** 단순과거 **06** 현재완료진행
> **07** 현재진행 **08** 미래진행

Actual Test p.31

1 ⑤ **2** ② **3** ④ **4** ④ **5** ⑤ **6** ① **7** ④
8 have you been doing **9** did you call me
10 I will be running the ground

---

1 this time tomorrow가 온 것으로 보아, 미래형진행이 되어야 한다.

2 현재 진행형의 부정은 be동사 뒤에 not을 쓴다.

3 내가 사무실로 돌아오기 이전부터 계속된 상황이므로 과거완료 진행형인 had been working가 옳다.

4 현재완료 의문문에 대한 답이다.

5 문장에 since(~이래로)가 있으므로 (A)에는 현재완료가 적절하고, (B)에는 단순과거 시제로 쓰여야 한다.

6 so far(여태껏)가 온 것으로 보아, 현재완료 계속적 용법으로 쓰였다. 따라서 ①의 had been waiting은 have

been waiting이 되어야 한다.

7 ④는 과거진행형인 were watching이 되어야 한다.

8 '어떻게 지냈니?'란 의미로 How have you been doing?의 완료진행형의 의문문을 쓸 수 있다.

9 앞에 의문사 why가 있으므로 뒤에는 「주어＋동사＋목적어」 순이 된다.

10 다음 주 화요일, 즉 미래에 대한 이야기를 하고 있으므로 미래진행형으로 쓴다.

Review Test pp.32-34

01 ② **02** ④ **03** ⑤ **04** ① **05** ③ **06** ⑤
07 ① **08** ⑤ **09** ③ **10** ⑤ **11** ③ **12** ⑤
13 ③ **14** ② **15** ④ **16** ③ **17** Anthony
had cut the lawn **18** The twins have sung
in the choir for three years **19** Will you
have been eating **20** ⑤ **21** ④ **22** is →
was **23** have missing → have missed
24 ⑤ **25** haven't changed

---

01 매일 아침의 습관을 나타내는 현재시제가 들어가며, 주어가 Jane(3인칭 단수 여자)이므로 feeds가 알맞다.

02 yesterday로 보아, 과거형이 들어가야 한다.

03 right now로 보아 지금 현재 진행 중인 일이므로 현재진행형이 들어간다.

04 all day가 있으므로 현재 완료형이 들어간다.

05 last night이 있으므로 과거형 또는 과거 진행형이 들어간다.

06 tomorrow morning이 있으므로 미래 시제가 되어야한다. ⑤의 미래완료는 「by＋미래시점」과 함께 쓰이므로 적절하지 않다.

07 주어가 Children으로 복수이므로 ①의 has는 have가 되어야 한다.

08 현재완료는 「have[has]＋p.p.」형이므로 ⑤의 has being은 has been이 되어야 한다.

09 미래완료는 「will＋have＋p.p.」형이므로 ③의 had는 have가 되어야 한다.

10 ⑤는 미래완료이다. ① had won → will win, ② is blowing → blew, ③ will be brushing → was brushing, ④ worked → is working

11 ③은 과거 진행형이다. ① was → am, ② hasn't fed → will not feed, ④ take → took, ⑤ didn't → won't

12 ⑤는 반복되는 일을 나타내는 현재시제이다. ① is → was, ② will be leaving → left, ③ had been watching → is watching, ④ has given → will give

13 (A)에는 현재까지 계속되는 일을 나타내는 현재완료와 (B)는 현재 진행중인 일을 나타내는 현재진행형이 되어야 한다.

14 (A), (B)는 현재까지의 경험을 나타내는 현재완료가 되어야 한다.

15 첫 문장은 현재완료의 완료 용법으로, 두 번째 문장은 '가지다'는 의미로 일반동사 has가 들어간다.

16 둘 다 미래의 특정 시점에 진행되고 있을 일을 나타내므로 미래진행형을 쓴다.

17 「주어+had+p.p.~」의 과거완료 문장이다.

18 「주어+have+p.p.~」의 현재완료 문장이다.

19 「Will+주어+have been+-ing~?」의 미래완료 진행형 의문문이다.

20 과거진행형의 의미이므로 was looking이 된다.

21 과거완료 진행형의 의미이므로 had been talking이 된다.

22 last month로 보아, 과거시제이므로 is는 was가 되어야 한다.

23 현재완료는 「have+p.p.」 형태로 쓴다.

24 60년대의 상황을 말하므로 과거시제가 되어야 한다. 따라서 ⑤는 took이 되어야 한다.

25 문맥상 현재까지 '바뀌지 않았다'는 의미가 되어야 자연스러우므로, 현재완료 부정형 haven't changed로 써야 한다.

UNIT 06 | 조동사 1 (능력/허가/추측/의무)

p.36

해석 A: 부자들은 돈을 많이 쓸 수 있어.

B: 나는 그들이 그러면 안 된다고 생각해. 그들은 가난한 사람들에게 돈을 주어야 해.

Check up 1

p.37

A 01 Can 02 should 03 may 04 may not 05 should 06 ought to 07 cannot 08 must 09 can 10 might

B 01 have to 02 was 03 might leave 04 You'd better not 05 cannot be 06 Are 07 must see[has to see] 08 might have 09 should not throw 10 cross

---

A

01 잠시 당신의 휴대폰을 써도 될까요?

02 여러분은 여름에 자외선 차단제를 발라야만 합니다.

03 나는 그 남자가 인도에서 왔을지도 모른다고 생각한다.

04 당신은 신분증 없이는 이 건물에 들어올 수 없습니다.

05 우리 아버지는 내가 최선을 다했다는 것을 알아야만 한다.

06 나는 아버지에게 담배를 끊는 편이 좋겠다고 말했다.

07 우리가 경기에 졌다는 건 사실일 리가 없어.

08 해외여행을 하고 싶다면 너는 여권이 있어야 해.

09 여러분은 수업 후에 문자 메시지를 보내도 좋습니다.

10 그 영화는 아이들에게는 어려울 수도 있습니다.

> **해설** 01 허락 02 의무 03 추측 04 허락 05 의무 06 조언 07 강한 추측 08 의무 09 허락 10 추측

B

01 파티에 제 음식을 꼭 가져가야 하나요?

02 남자는 제시간에 기차를 탈 수 있었다.

03 그는 병 때문에 우리 축구팀을 떠날지도 모른다.

04 너는 내일 그에게 전화를 하지 않는 게 좋다.

05 그가 가방을 훔쳤다는 소문은 사실일 리가 없어.

06 너는 이 수학 문제를 풀 수 있니?

07 그가 지금 당장 의사의 진료를 받아야 한다고 생각해.

08 그는 매우 친절하기 때문에 친구가 많을 것이다.

09 너는 쓰레기를 버리면 안 돼.

10 지금 길을 건너도 되나요?

> **해설** 01 의무 02 능력 (과거) 03 추측 04 조언 (부정형) 05 강한 추측 06 능력 07 의무 08 추측 09 의무 (부정형) 10 허락

Check up 2

p.38

A 01 should not bite 02 may like 03 ought to quit 04 had better tie 05 might be awake 06 might need

B 01 may I take a rest 02 can go to school 03 might get sick 04 should be kept 05 must play football 06 can let you stay 07 you had better ask

---

A

01 나는 손톱을 물어뜯으면 안 된다. 왜냐하면 가끔씩 아프기 때문이다.

02 우리 할머니는 수다스럽다. 그녀는 말하는 것을 매우 좋좋아하는 것 같다.

03 우리 아버지는 건강을 위해 담배를 끊어야 한다.

04 우리 어머니는 요리할 때 머리를 묶어야 한다. 나는 가끔 음식에서 어머니 머리카락을 발견한다.

05 우리 누나는 커피를 너무 많이 마셔서, 나는 그녀가 밤에 깨어 있을 거라 생각한다.

06 우리 형은 스스로 심하게 긁기 때문에 의사에게 진료를 받아야 할 것 같다.

> **해설** 01 조언 02 추측 03 의무 04 조언 05 추측 06 추측

B

아들: 엄마, 오늘 집에서 쉬어도 돼요?

엄마: 글쎄, 오늘은 네가 학교에 갈 수 있을 것 같구나. 열이
없어.

아들: 하지만 나중에 아플 수도 있잖아요. 저는 내일 축구
시합에 나가야 하기 때문에 좋은 컨디션을 유지해야
만 해요. 아무도 저를 대신할 수 없단 말이에요.

엄마: 흠, 좋아. 오늘은 널 집에 있게 해줄 수 있어. 하지만
친구들에게 오늘 배운 것을 물어봐야만 해.

> 해설 01 허락 02 가능성 03 추측 04 의무 05 의무
> 06 허락 07 조언(의무)

Actual Test
p.39

1 ④   2 ⑤   3 ③   4 ③   5 ⑤   6 ⑤   7 ⑤

8 We had better prepare for global warming.

9 A helicopter is able to stay at one point.

10 May I leave early today?

---

1 may는 추측의 의미를 나타내므로 might를 대신 쓸 수
있다.

2 조언의 의미를 나타내는 조동사가 들어가야 한다.

3 be able to가 can을 대신해 쓰이는 것이므로, cannot
speak 또는 is not be able to speak이 되어야 한다.

4 주어진 문장의 might은 추측의 의미를 나타내며, ③의
could 역시 추측을 나타낸다.

5 have to가 must를 대신해 쓰이는 것이므로, you must
leave나 you have to leave가 되어야 한다.

6 be able to뒤에는 동사원형이 오므로 ⑤는 touch가
되어야 한다.

7 ⑤는 '지금쯤이면 마을을 빠져나가야만 한다' 는 의무
의 의미를 나타내지만 나머지 문장은 추측의 의미이다.

8 had better는 should와 같은 조언의 의미이다.

9 be able to는 can 대신 쓰여 능력의 의미를 갖는다.

10 허락을 나타내는 may로 대답했으므로 허락을 구하는
May로 물어야 한다.

UNIT 07 | 조동사 2 (미래/의지/과거 습관/부탁)
p.40

해석 A: 너 이 상자들 모두 옮길 거니?

B: 그래야 하는데 도움이 필요해. 네가 나를 도와 주겠니?

Check up 1
p.41

A 01 will study   02 will not be   03 is going
to go   04 are going to   05 could come
06 would visit   07 used to give   08 Would
09 give   10 used to send

B 01 are going to visit   02 would do well
03 used to go to concerts   04 Can you
keep   05 is going to make   06 The family
used to live   07 Are we going to have
08 used to be   09 Could you buy me

A

01 Jed는 대학에서 법이나 경영을 공부할 것이다.

02 나는 John이 내일 저녁에 이곳에 있지 않을 거라고 확
신한다.

03 우리 가족은 이번 여름에 캠핑을 갈 것이다.

04 나는 그들이 다음 기차를 탈 거라고 생각해.

05 그는 그 당시에 집에 매우 늦게 왔을 수 있다.

06 이모는 우리 생일에 우리를 보러 오곤 했다.

07 Ms. Smith는 방과후에 학생들에게 보충
수업을 하곤 했다.

08 탁자 위에 있는 설탕 좀 건네줄래요?

09 결정 전에 제게 생각할 시간을 좀 줄 수 있나요?

10 우리 학교는 좋은 대학교에 학생들을 많이 보내곤 했다.

> 해설 01 미래시제 02 조동사의 부정: 조동사＋not＋
> 동사원형 03-04 be going to＋동사원형 05-06 조동
> 사＋동사원형 07 조동사(used to)＋동사원형 08-09
> 조동사 의문문: 조동사＋주어＋동사원형 10 조동사＋동
> 사원형

B

01 미국에서 내 친척들이 다음 주에 나를 보러 올 것이다.

02 Joe는 수학 시험을 잘 보곤 했다.

03 나는 매 주말마다 오빠와 공연을 보러 가곤 했다.

04 나를 위해 내 비밀을 지켜줄 수 있겠니?

05 너무 많은 지방은 널 살찌게 만들 거야.

06 그 가족은 3년 전 중국에 살았었다.

07 우리는 오늘 밤 이곳에서 저녁을 먹을 건가요?

08 내가 어렸을 때 그 나무는 작았었다.

09 집에 오기 전에 시리얼과 우유를 사올 수 있나요?

> 해설 **01** 미래 **02** 과거 습관 **03** 과거 습관 **04** 부탁
> **05** 미래 **06** 과거 습관 **07** 미래 **08** 과거 습관 **09** 부탁

Check up 2
p.42

A **01** used to be **02** will have[is going to have] **03** will come[are going to come] **04** will build[is going to build] **05** would buy **06** would enjoy **07** used to be **08** will have[is going to have]

B **01** used to go to your theater **02** used to be very clean **03** Would you clean the restroom **04** used to impress me **05** you are not going to solve **06** I will complain

---

A

01 과거에는 5만 명의 사람들이 있었다.

02 미래에 그 도시에 50만 명의 사람들이 있을 것이다.

03 미래에 더 많은 사람들이 그 도시로 올 것이다.

04 그 도시는 내년에 복합건물을 지을 것이다.

05 사람들은 작은 지역 시장에서 물건을 사곤 했다.

06 사람들은 도시의 아이스링크에서 스케이트를 즐기곤 했다.

07 도시에 야구장이 있었으나, 지금은 없다.

08 그 도시에는 올림픽 경기장이 생길 것이다.

> 해설 **01** 과거의 사실 **02** 미래 **03** 미래 **04** 미래 **05**
> 과거의 사실 **06** 과거의 사실 **07** 과거의 사실 **08** 미래

B

Cinephil 극장 매니저 귀하

저는 당신의 극장에 자주 가곤 했는데, 지난 토요일 영화를 보러 갔을 때 넘어질 뻔했습니다. 바닥이 너무 끈적거렸습니다! 극장이 전에는 매우 깨끗했었습니다. 하지만 요즘에는 더럽고 위험합니다. 화장실도 지저분합니다. 저는 한 관리인에게 "지금 화장실 좀 치워 줄래요?"라고 말했습니다. 하지만 그는 저를 그냥 무시했습니다. 당신의 극장은 과거에는 나에게 깊은 인상을 줬지만, 이젠 더 이상 그렇지 않습니다. 만일 이 문제를 해결하지 못한다면, 나는 직접 정부 기관에 불만을 제기할 것입니다.

> 해설 **01** 과거의 사실 **02** 과거의 사실 **03** 부탁 **04** 과
> 거의 사실 **05** 미래 **06** 미래

Actual Test
p.43

1 ② **2** ④ **3** ④ **4** ② **5** ④ **6** ③ **7** ⑤

8 He used to be fat and unhealthy

9 Can you turn off the air conditioner for me

10 (A) used to sit   (B) would[used to] smile

---

1 used to 자체가 조동사로 쓰이므로, 앞에 be동사가 오지 않는다.

2 나머지는 모두 과거의 습관을 나타내지만 ④의 would는 '부탁'의 의미를 갖는다.

3 밑줄 친 would는 '과거의 습관, 상태'를 나타내며 이와 같은 의미로 쓰이는 것은 used to이다.

4 과거의 습관을 나타낼 때는 would나 used to를 쓴다. 부정형은 would not 또는 used not to를 쓴다.

5 조동사 would 뒤에는 동사원형 make가 온다.

6 '~하곤 했다'의 의미로 쓰이는 것은 used to이다. 따라서 ③은 used to take가 되어야 한다.

7 조동사 will을 써서 '부탁'의 의미를 나타낼 수 있다.

8 「주어＋조동사＋동사원형 ~」순으로 쓰면 된다.

9 조동사 의문문은 「조동사＋주어＋동사원형 ~?」순으로 쓴다.

10 (A) '앉아있곤 했다'는 과거의 상태를 나타내는 의미가 되어야 하므로 used to가 쓰인다. (B) '웃곤 했다'는 과거의 상태나 습관을 나타내므로, used to나 would가 쓰일 수 있다.

해석 Sam은 버스를 잘못 탔다.

그는 버스 번호를 확인했어야 했다.

그는 매우 바빴던 것 같다.

Check up 1 p.45

A 01 should have called 02 may have fixed 03 might have hidden 04 must have touched 05 could have asked 06 should not have waited 07 could have told 08 cannot have taken

B 01 should have seen a doctor 02 could have arrived in Seoul early 03 might have been thirsty 04 may not have driven the car 05 may not have been in Busan 06 might have melted 07 cannot have written the email 08 must have snowed hard last night

A

01 너는 경찰을 먼저 불렀어야 했어.

02 아버지는 어제 차를 수리하셨을지도 모른다.

03 그 고양이는 벽장 안에 숨어 있었을지도 모른다.

04 그 축구 선수는 손으로 공을 만졌던 것이 확실하다.

05 나는 Ann에게 보고서를 도와달라고 부탁할 수 있었다.

06 우리는 비가 그치기를 기다리지 말았어야 했다.

07 너는 진실을 말할 수도 있었지만, 내게 거짓말을 했어.

08 Sam이 이 사진을 직접 찍었을 리가 없다.

> **해설** 01 과거에 대한 후회 02 과거에 대한 추측 03 과거에 대한 추측 04 과거에 대한 강한 추측 05 과거에 할 수 있었던 일 06 과거에 대한 후회 07 과거에 할 수 있었던 일 08 과거에 대한 강한 추측

B

01 나는 배가 아팠지만 의사에게 가지 않았다.
  → 나는 배가 아파서 의사를 보러 갔어야만 했다.

02 기차가 제시간에 오지 않아서 나는 서울에 일찍 도착할 수 없었다.
  → 기차가 제시간에 왔더라면 나는 서울에 일찍 도착할 수 있었을 것이다.

03 그녀가 목마를 거라 생각했기 때문에, 나는 그녀에게 물을 가져다 주었다.
  → 나는 그녀가 목마를 것 같아서 나는 그녀에게 물을 가져다 주었다.

04 John은 술이 취했기 때문에, 나는 그가 차를 직접 몰지 않았을 거라고 생각한다.
  → 술이 취했기 때문에, John은 직접 차를 몰지 않았을 것이다.

05 그녀는 그 비행기를 탔기 때문에 부산에 있었다.
  → 그녀는 그 비행기를 타지 않았더라면 부산에 없었을 지도 모른다.

06 4월이었기 때문에 나는 산 위의 눈이 녹았을 거라고 생각했다.
  → 4월이기 때문에 산 위의 눈이 녹았을지도 모른다.

07 Jay는 자고 있었기 때문에, 나는 그가 그 이메일을 쓸 수 없었다고 확신했다.
  → Jay는 자고 있었기 때문에 그 이메일을 썼을 리가 없다.

08 길이 얼어 있다. 나는 어젯밤에 눈이 많이 왔을 거라고 생각한다.
  → 길이 얼어 있기 때문에, 지난밤에는 눈이 많이 왔었음이 틀림없다.

> **해설** 01 과거에 대한 후회 02 과거에 일어날 수 있었던 일 03 과거에 대한 추측 04 과거에 대한 추측 (부정형) 05 과거에 대한 추측 (부정형) 06 과거에 대한 추측 07 과거에 대한 강한 추측 08 과거에 대한 강한 추측

Check up 2 p.46

A 01 should not have been 02 could have chosen 03 should have listened 04 could have bought 05 should have prepared 06 could have stood 07 should have gone 08 could have seen

B 01 must have stayed up 02 may have gone 03 might have left 04 may have forgotten 05 must have been

A

01 Peggy는 오늘 학교에 늦지 않았어야 했다.

02 Peggy는 학교 소풍을 어디로 갈지 결정할 수도 있었다.

03 Jack은 Paul의 충고를 들었어야 했다.

04 Jack은 최신 게임 CD를 반 가격에 살 수도 있었다.

05 Jane은 오늘 아침 일찍 콘서트를 준비했어야만 했다.

06 Jane은 무대 위에 있는 가수 바로 앞에 설 수도 있었다.

07 Paul은 지난밤에 일찍 잤어야만 했다.

08 Paul은 해변의 아름다운 일출을 볼 수도 있었다.

> **해설** **01** 과거에 대한 후회 **02** 과거에 할 수 있었던 일
> **03** 과거에 대한 후회 **04** 과거에 할 수 있었던 일 **05** 과
> 거에 대한 후회 **06** 과거에 할 수 있었던 일 **07** 과거에
> 대한 후회 **08** 과거에 할 수 있었던 일

B

학급의 점심시간이다. Paula는 자리에 앉아서 잠에 들었
다. 그녀는 어젯밤에 늦게까지 깨어 있었던 것이 분명하다.
George는 친구를 만나러 교실 밖으로 나갔다. 그는 옆반의
John을 만나러 갔을 것이다. Marie는 선생님께 밖에 한 시
간만 나갔다 오겠다고 부탁했다. 그녀는 집에 숙제를 두고
왔을 수도 있다. Peter와 Lisa는 구내식당에 가는 길이다.
그들은 오늘 아침에 점심 가져오는 것을 깜박했을지도 모른
다. Sam은 점심을 매우 빨리 먹고 있다. 그는 오늘 오전 배
가 많이 고팠던 것이 분명하다.

> **해설** **01** 과거에 대한 강한 추측 **02** 과거에 대한 추측
> **03** 과거에 대한 추측 **04** 과거에 대한 추측 **05** 과거에
> 대한 강한 추측

■ Actual Test ■   p.47

1 ① **2** ⑤ **3** ③ **4** ③ **5** ⑤ **6** ④ **7** ⑤

8 He cannot have ignored my call. **9** The staff could have turned down the volume. **10** must have spent

---

1 조동사의 과거형은 「조동사＋have p.p.」형태로, leave
는 p.p.형태인 left가 되어야 한다.

2 should의 과거형 부정은 「shouldn't＋have p.p.」형
태가 되어야 한다.

3 과거에 할 수도 있었던 일을 나타내므로 「could＋
have p.p.」가 쓰여야 한다.

4 둘 다 「조동사＋have p.p.」형으로 (A)에는 be동사의
p.p.인 been과 (B)에는 bring의 p.p.인 bought이 들어가
야 한다.

5 「should＋have p.p.」 형태로 '더 조심했어야 했다'는
과거에 대한 후회를 나타내는 말이 들어가야 자연스럽다.

6 조동사의 과거는 「조동사＋have p.p.」로 나타내므로,
④는 written이 되어야 한다.

7 조동사 과거형의 부정은 「조동사＋not＋have p.p.」
로 나타내므로, ⑤는 not have bought이 되어야 한다.

8-9 「주어＋조동사＋have p.p.~」순으로 쓴다.

10 문맥상 과거 사실에 대한 강한 추측을 나타내는 말이
와야 하므로, 「must＋have p.p.」형으로 쓴다.

■ Review Test ■   pp.48–50

01 ① **02** ④ **03** ⑤ **04** ③ **05** ⑤ **06** ③
07 ① **08** ③ **09** ② **10** ③ **11** ④ **12** ④
13 ② **14** ① **15** ② **16** ② **17** ③ **18** ④
19 could have saved the patient **20** Our bodies are able to change **21** Martha used to live with her family **22** been → be **23** should had paid → should have paid **24** ③ **25** should have finished

---

01 조동사 뒤에는 동사원형을 쓴다.

02 조동사 의문문은 「조동사＋주어＋동사원형」순이 된다.

03 조동사의 과거는 「조동사＋have p.p.」형태이다.

04 빈칸에는 조동사의 과거가 들어가야 한다. could not
뒤에는 동사원형이 와야 하므로 빈칸에 올 수 없다.

05 빈칸에는 will, can, would, could 등, '부탁'의 의미
를 나타내는 조동사가 들어간다.

06 빈칸 뒤에 동사원형이 나오므로, 빈칸에는 조동사가 들
어가야 한다. 조동사의 과거형은 뒤에 have p.p.가 오므로
빈칸에 들어갈 수 없다.

07 조동사의 과거는 「조동사＋have p.p.」이므로 ①은
He might have made ~가 되어야 한다.

08 조동사 뒤에는 동사원형이 와야 하므로 ③은 would win이 되어야 한다.

09 조동사의 부정형은 조동사 뒤에 not을 붙이므로, ②는 might not be가 되어야 한다.

10 오븐에 있는 빵이 맛있을 거라는 추측의 의미로 might는 may로 바꾸어 쓸 수 있다.

11 '라디오를 듣곤 했다'는 과거의 습관을 나타낸다. 과거의 습관은 would 또는 used to를 쓴다.

12 (A)에는 '부탁'의 의미를 갖는 could가, (B)에는 be able to가 쓰여 are가 들어가야 한다.

13 (A)에는 '~일 리 없다'는 강한 추측을 나타내는 cannot이, (B)에는 미래를 나타내는 be going to가 쓰여 3인칭 단수 주어에 맞는 is가 들어가야 한다.

14 밑줄 친 may는 허락의 의미로 can으로 바꾸어 쓸 수 있다.

15 밑줄 친 부분은 조동사의 과거로 과거에 대한 추측을 나타낸다. 조동사 might은 may로 바꾸어 쓸 수 있다.

16 조동사 could는 능력, 가능을 나타내는 can의 과거형이다.

17 '~하지 말았어야 했다'는 과거에 대한 후회를 나타내므로 「shouldn't + have p.p.」가 쓰여야 한다.

18 과거의 상태, 습관을 나타내므로 used to가 쓰여야 한다.

19 「조동사 + have p.p.」의 형태가 되어야 한다.

20 능력을 나타내는 「be able to + 동사원형」으로 쓴다.

21 「주어 + used to + 동사원형」의 순서가 되어야 한다.

22 조동사 used to 뒤에는 동사원형이 와야 하므로 been은 be로 바꾼다.

23 「should + have p.p.」의 형태가 되어야 하므로 ①의 had는 have로 바꾼다.

24 should는 '~해야 한다'는 의무의 뜻을 가지고 있으며, have to로 바꾸어 쓸 수 있다.

25 '어제 보고서를 끝냈어야 했다'는 의미를 나타내야 하므로, 「should + have p.p.」의 형태가 되어야 한다.

UNIT **09** | to부정사의 쓰임 p.52

해석 A: 함께 이 보드게임을 하고 싶니?
B: 하고 싶지만, 그 게임을 어떻게 하는지 몰라.
A: 걱정하지마. 배우기 쉬워.

🌣 Check up 1 p.53

A 01 부사 02 명사 03 명사 04 형용사 05 부사
06 명사 07 형용사 08 명사 09 형용사 10 부사

B 01 what to do 02 how to use 03 when to take 04 where to celebrate 05 how to turn 06 whether to buy 07 what to discuss 08 which flower to buy 09 whether to build 10 which way to go

A

01 나는 바닥에 있는 신문을 줍기 위해 몸을 굽혔다.
02 그들은 그에게 전화를 걸어 질문을 하고 싶었다.
03 야생 동물을 연구하는 것은 나에게 재미있어 보였다.
04 당신에게는 이 건물에 들어올 허가가 없다.
05 우리는 큰 비를 피하려고 안에 머물렀다.
06 그때 공군에 들어가는 것은 나에게는 위험했다.
07 너는 나와 함께 갤러리에 갈 시간이 있니?
08 그녀의 직업은 높은 빌딩 바깥쪽 창문을 닦는 것이다.
09 농부들에게는 밭에 뿌릴 충분한 물이 필요하다.
10 그는 엄마를 만나는 것을 피하기 위해 건물로 돌아갔다.

> **해설** 01 부사: 동사 bent 수식 02 명사: want의 목적어 03 명사: 주어 04 형용사: 명사 permission 수식 05 부사: 동사 stay 수식 06 명사: 가주어 07 형용사: 명사 time 수식 08 명사: 보어 09 형용사: 명사 water 수식 10 부사: 동사 went 수식

B

01 네가 자라서 무얼 하게 될지는 알기 어렵다.
02 아무도 나에게 이 아이스크림 기계를 쓰는 법을 알려주지 않았다.

03 나는 언제 비행기를 타고 고향에 돌아가야 할지 잊어버렸다.
04 우리는 엄마의 생일을 어디서 축하할지 알아봐야 해.
05 그녀는 전등을 끄는 방법을 모른다.
06 Jack에게 이 책을 살지 말지 물어봐 줄래?
07 학생들은 무엇을 논의해야 할지 몰랐다.
08 그는 그녀를 위해 어떤 꽃을 사야 할지 알 수 없었다.
09 그들은 댐을 지을지 말지 결정하지 못했다.
10 나는 교차로에서 어느 쪽으로 가야 할지 결정했다.

> **해설** 01 무엇을 할지 02 어떻게 쓰는지 03 언제 탈지 04 어디서 축하할지 05 어떻게 끌지 06 살지 (말지) 07 무엇을 논의할지 08 어떤 꽃을 살지 09 지을지 (말지) 10 어느 쪽으로 갈지

🌣 Check up 2 p.54

A 01 To watch soccer matches 02 to observe the beautiful aurora 03 to enjoy sunbathing 04 To enjoy cold weather 05 to take pictures of the Taj Mahal 06 to hike through the mountains

B 01 protect[to protect] 02 not to harm 03 what to do 04 to explore 05 to capture 06 whether to sign

A

01 리버풀에서 축구 경기를 보는 것은 내 소망 중 하나이다.
02 오슬로에서 아름다운 오로라를 관찰하는 것은 틀림없이 재미있을 것이다.
03 나는 나폴리에서 일광욕을 즐기고 싶다.
04 모스크바에서 추운 날씨를 즐기는 것은 힘들겠지만 재미있을 것이다.
05 아그라에서 나는 타지마할의 사진을 찍고 싶다.
06 카트만두에 있는 산을 등반하는 것은 피곤하겠지만, 나는 그곳에 가고 싶다.

B

여러 사람들이 미국의 옐로우스톤 국립공원을 보호하는 것을 도왔습니다. 1600년대와 1700년대에 몇몇 사냥꾼들은 동물의 털을 얻기 위해서 그곳으로 갔습니다. 그들은 그 아름다운 곳을 해치러 간 것은 아니었기 때문에, 경이로운 경관들을 보느라 며칠을 보냈습니다. 그때 그들은 그것에 대해 무엇을 할지 알았습니다. 그들이 마을로 돌아왔을 때 그들은 그 산에 대해 이야기 했습니다. 사람들은 옐로우스톤을 탐험하고 싶어했고, 사진가인 Ferdinand Hayden과 한 예술가가 옐로우스톤의 아름다움을 담기 위해 그곳에 갔습니다. 그들은 그 사진을 의회에 보여주었습니다. Grant 대통령은 법안에 서명을 할지 결정을 해야 했고, 그는 옐로우스톤을 미국의 첫 번째 국립공원으로 지정했습니다.

Actual Test
p.55

1 ③ **2** ③ **3** ④ **4** ② **5** ② **6** ① **7** ③
8 will be happy to hear **9** stopped to think of how to cross **10** to make

1 앞에 나온 things를 수식하는 형용사적 용법이다.

2 밑줄 친 부분은 '〜하기 위해'를 뜻하는 부사적 용법의 목적을 나타낸다. ③도 '낮잠을 자기 위해'의 의미로 같은 용법으로 쓰였다.

3 ④는 '〜하기 위해'를 뜻하는 부사적 용법이며, 나머지는 모두 앞의 명사를 수식하는 형용사적 용법이다.

4 to부정사의 부정형은 「not + to부정사」이므로 to not have는 not to have가 되어야 한다.

5 (A)는 「which + 명사 + to부정사」, (B)는 「how + to부정사」의 형태이다.

6 문맥상 watch는 '〜하는 것'의 의미로 보어 자리에 쓰였으므로 to watch가 되어야 한다.

7 need는 to부정사 목적어를 취하고 outgoing은 형용사이므로 사이에 be동사의 원형인 be가 와야 한다.

8 to부정사 부사적 용법의 감정의 원인을 나타내므로 「형용사 + to부정사」의 순서로 쓰인다.

9 「동사 + to부정사」, 「how + to부정사」의 순서로 쓰인다.

10 '캠프를 할 완벽한 장소'라는 의미로 앞의 spot을 수식하는 형용사적 용법으로 사용된 to부정사 형태가 쓰인다.

UNIT 10 | 동명사의 쓰임
p.56

해석 외국어를 배우는 것은 재미있습니다.
나는 영어로 외국인들과 이야기하는 것이 좋습니다.
여러분은 어떤가요? 여러분도 외국어 배우는 것을 좋아하나요?

Check up 1
p.57

A **01** 주어 **02** 목적어 **03** 목적어 **04** 보어 **05** 목적어 **06** 주어 **07** 목적어 **08** 보어 **09** 주어 **10** 주어

B **01** I **02** my **03** The athlete **04** I **05** Uncle Sam **06** his **07** The mosquitoes **08** your father **09** Nobody **10** Jenny's

A

01 애완동물을 기르는 것은 아이들에게 도움이 될 수 있다.

02 나는 아침 일찍 조깅하는 것을 좋아한다.

03 George는 그의 개들을 사람들에게 보여주는 것을 즐겼다.

04 우리가 할 수 있는 유일한 일은 경찰을 기다리는 것뿐이다.

05 Ava는 새 옷을 사기 위해 돈을 모으기 시작했다.

06 많이 걷는 것은 좋은 운동이 될 수 있다.

07 많은 사람들이 돈 버는 데에 관심이 있다.

08 큰 이슈는 회사의 빚을 줄이는 것이다.

09 드라이브를 오래 하는 것은 사람들을 피곤하게 한다.

10 야채를 충분히 먹지 않는 것은 네 건강에 좋지 않아.

B

01 나는 나의 오랜 친구를 만나는 것이 좋았다.

02 그는 주말에 할 일로 내가 차고를 청소하도록 허락했다.

03 그 선수는 배영을 잘한다.

04 나는 직업으로 제트기를 조정하는 것을 고려 중이다.

05 Sam 삼촌은 그 큰 물고기를 잡는 것을 즐겼다.

06 그녀는 그가 밤 10시 이후에 집에 오는 것을 걱정하지 않니?

07 모기들은 마침내 나를 물어뜯는 걸 멈췄다.

08 너희 아버지는 강에서 낚시하는 것을 즐기시니?

09 아무도 화장실 청소를 좋아하지 않는다.

10 그녀의 어머니는 Jenny가 춤을 배우는 것을 부끄러워하신다.

🍀 Check up 2
p.58

A **01** planting various trees **02** caring for the plants in her garden **03** Selling his stuff at high prices **04** trading baseball cards **05** playing the cello **06** Flying kites at the park **07** writing short stories **08** riding the roller coaster

B **01** inviting **02** cooking **03** going **04** arriving **05** picking **06** mixing **07** adding **08** making

---

A

01 Lisa는 정원에 다양한 나무를 기르는 것에 소질이 있다.

02 Lisa는 정원에 있는 나무를 돌보는 것을 좋아한다.

03 자기 물건을 높은 가격에 파는 것이 Jerry가 잘하는 일이다.

04 Jerry의 취미는 야구 카드를 교환하는 것이다.

05 Maria는 첼로 연주를 잘하는 것을 자랑스러워 한다.

06 공원에서 연을 날리는 것은 Maria가 가장 좋아하는 취미이다.

07 Paul은 단편 이야기 쓰는 것에 흥미가 있으며, 그는 그것들을 매우 잘 쓴다.

08 Paul은 놀이 공원에서 롤러코스터 타는 것을 종종 즐긴다.

B

어제 Jacobson 이모는 조카인 Kelly를 집으로 초대하고 싶었다. 그들은 함께 요리하는 데에 익숙했다. Kelly는 이모의 전화를 받고 나서 이모네 집에 가는 것을 기대하고 있었다. 이모네 집에 도착하자마자, Kelly는 부엌으로 갔다. 이모는 초콜릿 케이크와 쿠키를 굽고 있었다. Kelly는 이모가 만든 쿠키를 집어 들지 않을 수 없었다. 이모는 Kelly에게 밀가루와 계란을 잘 섞으라고 했지만, Kelly는 둘을 섞는 데 어려움을 겪었다. 반죽이 너무 달았지만 그때는 밀가루를 더 넣는 것이 소용이 없었다. 마침내 Kelly와 이모는 요리를 마쳤다. 그들은 케이크와 쿠키를 만들면서 좋은 시간을 보냈다.

Actual Test
p.59

1 ④ **2** ⑤ **3** ② **4** ③ **5** ② **6** ④ **7** ⑤
8 Not having much fruit **9** buying unhealthy snacks **10** he was having difficulty training

---

1 동사 enjoy는 뒤에 목적어로 동명사가 온다.

2 밑줄 친 동명사는 동사 began의 목적어이며, ⑤의 dropping도 동사 remember의 목적어이다.

3 ②에서 동명사의 의미상 주어는 his dog이다.

4 동명사의 부정은 「not/never ＋ -ing」이다. 따라서 ③의 Following not은 Not following이 되어야 한다.

5 ②의 become은 becoming 또는 to become이 되어 주격보어의 역할을 해야 한다.

6 동사 hate의 목적어로, 동사원형이 아닌 동명사를 취하므로 listen은 listening이 되어야 한다.

7 cannot help -ing는 '~하지 않을 수 없다'는 의미이다.

8 동명사의 부정형은 앞에 not을 붙이므로 Not having ~이 되어야 한다.

9 「spend + 돈/시간 + -ing」의 형태가 된다. 동명사를 목적어로 갖는다.

10 have difficulty -ing는 '~하는 데 어려움이 있다'는 의미이다.

UNIT **11** | to부정사와 동명사 p.60

해석 A: 너는 내 생일날 나에게 전화하는 걸 잊었어.

B: 정말? 하지만 나는 어젯밤에 너에게 전화한 게 기억나. 어제가 네 생일 아니었니?

A: 아니었어!

Check up 1 p.61

A **01** to join **02** answering **03** to move, moving **04** to see **05** to watch, watching **06** speaking **07** going **08** to fall, falling

B **01** to feel **02** playing **03** to show **04** cooking **05** to take **06** to be **07** talking **08** to go **09** to cry[crying] **10** jogging

A

01 그 남자는 군대에 가기로 결심했다.

02 저희를 위해 전화를 받아주시면 실례가 될까요?

03 그 차는 길을 따라 천천히 움직이기 시작했다.

04 아무도 회의에서 그를 보리라 예상하지 않았다.

05 어떤 사람들은 공포 영화 보는 것을 싫어한다.

06 너는 내일 학급생들 앞에서 발표하는 것을 포기하면 안 돼.

07 집고양이들은 보통 밖으로 나가는 것을 피한다.

08 폭우가 내리기 시작했다.

해설 **01** decide + to부정사 **02** mind + 동명사 **03** begin + to부정사 / 동명사 **04** expect + to부정사 **05** hate + to부정사 / 동명사 **06** give up + 동명사 **07** avoid + 동명사 **08** start + to부정사 / 동명사

B

01 아이들은 오후 11시 이후에는 피곤해지기 쉽다.

02 매우 재미있었기 때문에. 그 게임은 할 만한 가치가 있었다.

03 나는 내 숙제를 보여주는 데 동의하지 않았다.

04 우리 엄마는 부엌에서 요리하느라 바빴다.

05 대부분의 학생들은 보통 시험 볼 준비가 되어 있지 않다.

06 나는 집에 혼자 있고 싶었지만. 아무도 나가지 않았다.

07 한 시간 뒤에 소녀는 마침내 말하기를 끝마쳤다.

08 남자는 오늘 교외로 나갈 계획이 없었다.

09 어린 소녀는 장난감 가게 안에서 울기 시작했다.

10 저녁에 조깅하는 것을 즐기니?

해설 **01** be likely + to부정사 **02** worth -ing **03** agree + to부정사 **04** be busy -ing **05** be ready + to부정사 **06** hope + to부정사 **07** finish + 동명사 **08** plan + to부정사 **09** start + to부정사/동명사 **10** enjoy + 동명사

Check up 2 p.62

A **01** locking **02** to calm **03** to listen **04** putting **05** watching

B **01** working **02** to hike[hiking] **03** o **04** to take **05** working **06** o **07** to cut **08** cutting

---

A

01 A: 우리가 나오기 전에 문을 잠궜니?
   B: 응. 내가 문을 잠궜던 게 기억나.

02 A: 왜 그렇게 아기가 크게 울지?
   B: 모르겠어. 한 시간 동안 달래려고 노력해 봤는데. 안 됐어.

03 A: 봐! 그 나라에 지진이 났어!
   B: 이런 천재지변이! 잠깐 멈춰서 뉴스를 들어보자.

04 A: 오, 우리 카트에 계란이 두 팩 들었네.
　　B: 미안, 카트에 이미 하나 넣었던 걸 깜박했어.

05 A: 우리 팝콘이랑 음료수가 다 떨어졌어.
　　B: 내가 가서 좀 가져올게. 잠깐 영화보는 걸 멈추자.

B

저는 수목 관리원이며, 숲에서 일하는 것을 좋아합니다. 나는 어렸을 때 하이킹을 시작했고, 숲에 있는 것이 매우 좋았습니다. 그때, 저는 삼림 돌보는 일을 제 직업으로 삼기로 결심했습니다. 저는 보통 밤이 오기 전에 일을 마칩니다. 하지만 저는 때때로 늦게까지 일을 하는데, 왜냐하면 몇몇 벌목꾼들은 저를 피해 밤에 나무를 베려고 계획하기 때문입니다. 가끔 저는 나무를 자르는 것에 개의치 않는데, 왜냐하면 그것이 숲을 건강하게 지켜주기 때문입니다. 하지만 벌목꾼들은 환경을 보호하는 법을 준수해야만 합니다.

> 해설　01 like＋동명사/to부정사　02 start＋to부정사/동명사　03 love＋to부정사/동명사　04 decide＋to부정사　05 finish＋동명사　06 try＋to부정사: ～하려고 애쓰다　07 plan＋to부정사　08 mind＋동명사

Actual Test　p.63

1 ③　2 ②　3 ⑤　4 ⑤　5 ⑤　6 ②　7 ④

8 You should not avoid talking to your parents.
9 Pets are worth raising with children.
10 start to try to do something

1　to부정사의 의미상의 주어는 「for＋to부정사」의 형태이다.

2　foolish 같은 사람의 성격을 나타내는 형용사가 올 때 의미상 주어는 「of＋to부정사」로 나타낸다.

3　decide는 to부정사를 목적어로 취한다.

4　consider는 동명사를 목적어로 취하므로 ⑤의 to join은 joining이 되어야 한다.

5　지난 여름에 '자전거를 탔던 사실'을 기억하냐고 물었으므로 「remember＋동명사」가 되어야 한다.

6　hope는 to부정사를 목적어로 취하므로 ②의 visiting은 to visit이 되어야 한다.

7　문맥상 '다리 떠는 것'을 멈추지 못한다는 뜻이므로 ④의 stop 뒤에는 동명사 shaking이 온다.

8　avoid는 동명사를 목적어로 취한다.

9　'～할 가치가 있다'는 뜻은 「be worth＋-ing」의 형태로 나타낸다.

10　'무언가를 하려 시도하기 시작한다'는 의미가 되어야 한다. start는 목적어로 동명사와 to부정사를 모두 취한다.

Review Test　p.64-66

01 ⑤　02 ④　03 ⑤　04 ②　05 ①　06 ⑤
07 ④　08 ④　09 ③　10 ④　11 ④　12 ②
13 ③　14 ④　15 ③　16 ⑤　17 ②　18 ⑤
19 tried to enter the abandoned house
20 need to consider what to do　21 hope to spend his time doing nothing　22 of → for
23 go → to go　24 ①　25 To communicate with the whales

01　'그의 생일 파티에 초대 할'이라는 의미로 to부정사의 형용사적 용법이 쓰여야 한다.

02　「be busy＋-ing」는 '～하느라 바쁘다'는 의미이다.

03　「how＋to부정사」는 '～하는 법'이라는 의미이다.

04　뒤에 「of＋목적격」이 왔으므로 빈칸에는 성격을 나타내는 형용사만 들어갈 수 있다.

05　what to fix는 '무엇을 고쳐야 할지'라는 의미이나, 이미 fix 뒤에 the chair라는 목적어가 있으므로 빈칸에 들어갈 수 없다.

06　「be likely＋to부정사」는 '～하기 쉽다'는 의미로 ⑤는 to be가 되어야 한다.

07　「be used to＋-ing」 형태가 되어야 하므로 ④는 is used to eating이 되어야 한다.

08　It is no use -ing의 형태가 되어야 하므로 ④의 regret은 regretting이 되어야 한다.

09　give up은 목적어로 동명사를 취하므로 ③의 to learn은 learning이 되어야 한다.

10　① to go → going, ② have → having, ③ to watch → watching, ⑤ to prepare → preparing

11　① visit → to visit, ② tasting → to taste, ③ buying → to buy, ⑤ telling → to tell

12　① to come → coming, ③ to drink → drinking, ④ to buy → buying, ⑤ to go → going

13 동사 like는 의미의 차이 없이 to부정사와 동명사 둘 다를 목적어로 취한다.

14 동사 enjoy는 동명사를 목적어로 취하므로 (A)에는 traveling, (B)는 문맥상 '걸었던 것'을 기억하냐고 묻는 것이므로 동명사 walking이 들어가야 한다.

15 동사 hope는 to부정사를 목적어로 취하므로 (A)에는 to talk, (B)는 「on + -ing」 형태가 되어야 하므로 seeing이 알맞다.

16 「whether + to부정사」는 '~할지 말지'의 의미이다.

17 「형용사 + for 목적격 + to부정사」의 형태가 되어야 한다.

18 「be likely + to부정사」는 '~하기 쉽다'는 의미이다.

19 「try + to부정사」는 '~하려고 노력하다'는 의미이다.

20 동사 need의 목적어로 to consider, consider의 목적어로 명사절 what to do가 온 형태이다.

21 동사 hope는 to부정사를 목적어로 취하며, 동사 spend는 뒤에 「시간/돈 + -ing」 형태를 취한다.

22 to부정사의 의미상 주어는 전치사 for를 써서 나타낸다.

23 동사 plan은 to부정사를 목적어로 취한다.

24 to stay는 '머물기 위해서'라는 의미로 ①과 같은 부사적 용법이다.

25 '고래와 의사소통하는 것'라는 의미로 to부정사의 명사적 용법이 쓰여 주어 자리에 와야 한다.

CHAPTER V 분사구문

UNIT 12 | 분사구문의 형태와 쓰임   p.68

해석 음악을 들으면서 나는 길을 걸어갔다.

길을 걸어가면서 나는 내 친구들을 보았다.

친구와 이야기하면서 나는 우리 엄마를 만났다.

☁ Check up 1   p.69

A 01 Finishing eating the main course
02 Keeping driving north   03 Picking the strawberries   04 Sitting on the airplane
05 Hurrying to get to the station   06 Not wanting to be late for the class

B 01 I read a book   02 he knew the answer to the question   03 he doesn't have many chances to meet foreigners   04 he spent all of his paycheck   05 I was not ready for the trip   06 he opened his new business

A

01 주요리를 먹은 후에 모든 사람들은 디저트를 먹었다.

02 북쪽으로 계속 운전해 가면 교차로에 도착할 것입니다.

03 딸기를 따면서 Maria는 노래를 불렀다.

04 비행기에 앉아서 Jane은 창 밖을 보았다.

05 역에 도착하기 위해 서둘렀지만 우리는 기차를 타지 못했다.

06 수업에 늦기 싫었기 때문에 그녀는 빨리 뛰기 시작했다.

> **해설** 01 시간 02 조건 03 부대상황 04 부대상황
> 05 양보 06 이유 (부정형)

B

01 책을 읽을 때, 나는 휴대폰을 끈다.

02 Jay는 그 문제에 대한 답을 알았음에도 불구하고 손을 들지 않았다.

03 Mr. Kim은 외국인을 만날 기회가 많이 없기 때문에 영어를 잘하지 못한다.

04 월급을 다 써버려서 그는 더 이상 돈이 없었다.

05 여행 준비가 되지 않아서 나는 칫솔을 챙기는 것을 잊었다.

06 새로운 사업을 시작하기 전에 Bob은 직장을 그만두었다.

> **해설** 01 시간 02 양보 03 이유 04 이유 05 이유
> 06 시간

☁ Check up 2   p.70

A 01 Failing to catch the bus   02 Waking up early   03 Not being able to hear the alarm   04 Riding in his father's car
05 Arguing with her mom   06 Spending too much time choosing clothes

B 01 feeling bored   02 entering the swamp
03 Looking dark   04 Not knowing
05 Moss hanging from their branches
06 Looking around   07 Hearing another splash   08 Shining his flashlight

A

01 버스를 잡지 못해서 Sunny는 화요일에 지각을 했다.

02 일찍 일어났기 때문에 Sunny는 수요일에 학교에 지각하지 않았다.

03 알람을 듣지 못해서 Jamie는 화요일에 지각을 했다.

04 아버지의 차를 타고 왔기 때문에 Jamie는 수요일에 학교에 제시간에 왔다.

05 엄마와 싸우느라 Jennifer는 화요일에 제시간에 올 수 없었다.

06 옷을 고르는 데 너무 많은 시간을 보내서 Jennifer는 수요일에도 지각을 했다.

> **해설** 03 분사문의 부정: not + 분사구문

B

지난 주말, Eric은 지루했기 때문에 늪을 통과하는 여행에 갔다. 보트의 운전사는 늪으로 들어가면서 속력을 낮추었다. 늪이 어두워 보여서 Eric은 약간 긴장했다. 어두운 물속

에 어떤 종류의 생물체가 숨어 있을지 몰랐기 때문에 그는 두려웠다. 이끼가 가지에 걸려 있어서 늪 주위의 나무는 거미줄처럼 보였다. 갑자기 그는 철썩거리는 큰 소리를 들었다. 주위를 둘러보았지만 그는 물속에서 아무것도 보지 못했다. 다시 한 번 철썩거리는 소리를 들은 후, 그는 물 가까이로 다가갔다. 어둠 속으로 전등을 비췄을 때 그는 악어의 꼬리를 보았다.

> **해설** **01** 이유 **02** 부대상황 **03** 이유 **04** 이유, 분사문의 부정: not + 분사구문 **05** 이유, 주절의 주어 ≠ 종속절의 주어 **06** 양보 **07** 시간 **08** 시간

Actual Test

1 ⑤　**2** ④　**3** ④　**4** ③　**5** ①　**6** ③　**7** ⑤
8 Checking the time　**9** Not being hungry
10 eating meat for their meals

1 빈칸에는 부사절이나 분사구문이 들어가야 한다.

2-3 밑줄 친 부사절의 「접속사 + 주어 + 동사」를 분사구문으로 바꾼다.

4 '음악을 들으면서' 는 부대상황의 분사구문을 나타낸다.

5 말을 '타면서' 석양을 본 것이므로 ridden은 능동의 의미인 riding이 되어야 한다.

6 분사구문을 부정할 때는 not이나 never를 분사 앞에 붙인다.

7 문맥상 '아빠를 보자' 의 의미가 되므로 시간을 나타내는 부사절을 쓴다.

8 주어를 생략하고, 동사 checked를 분사 checking으로 바꾼다.

9 동사 was를 분사 being으로 바꾼 후 앞에 not을 붙여 준다.

10 문맥상 '고기를 먹지만 사람들을 거의 해치지 않는다' 는 의미가 되어야 자연스럽다.

UNIT **13** | 다양한 분사구문

해석 운전을 하면서 Ellie는 친구로부터 온 전화를 받았다. 친구와 이야기를 하면서 그녀는 계속 운전했다. 비가 너무 많이 와서 그녀는 잠시 운전을 멈췄다.

Check up 1

A **01** While walking to the mall　**02** Since hurting his back at the football game
03 With his short hair blowing in the wind
04 After hearing how cold it was outside
05 With both its legs broken　**06** Although being good at public speaking

B **01** Joe finishing dinner　**02** The waiter coming to our table　**03** Jack trying to sleep last night　**04** It raining a lot in summer　**05** Sarah saying hello to him
06 There being no one at home

A

01 쇼핑몰로 가다가 나는 내 오랜 친구를 우연히 만났다.

02 축구 경기에서 등을 다쳤기 때문에 Alex는 병원에 있었다.

03 바람에 그의 짧은 머리가 흩날리면서, 그는 언덕에 잠시 서 있었다.

04 밖이 얼마나 추운지 들은 후로 나는 나가지 않기로 결정했다.

05 양쪽 다리가 모두 부러진 채로 그 새는 날 수 없었다.

06 대중 앞에서 말을 잘함에도 불구하고, 그는 회의에서 한 마디도 할 수 없었다.

> **해설** **01** while(~하면서): 시간 **02** since(~ 때문에): 이유 **03** with(~한 채로): 부대상황 **04** after(~후에): 시간 **05** with(~한 채로): 부대상황 **06** although(~에도 불구하고): 양보

B

01 Joe가 저녁 식사를 끝마쳤을 때, 전화가 울렸다.

02 웨이터가 우리 테이블로 오기 전에 나는 이미 쇠고기를 먹기로 결정했다.

03 Jack이 어젯밤에 잠을 청하려고 할 때, 모기가 계속 귓가에서 윙윙거렸다.

04 여름에는 비가 많이 와서 나는 항상 우산을 가지고 다닌다.

05 Sarah가 인사를 했음에도 불구하고 그는 Sarah를 알아보지 못했다.

06 집에 아무도 없었기 때문에 나는 직접 아침을 만들었다.

Check up 2 — p.74

A **01** It being cold there **02** People needing to get clean **03** There being children who need to study **04** There being no electricity **05** There being people who are hungry **06** People needing some clean water

B **01** Strictly speaking **02** considering that **03** Being young **04** Being outside **05** Although starting **06** When having free time **07** It being sunny **08** being the first people

---

A

01 그곳은 춥기 때문에 나는 그 지역에 담요를 보낼 것이다.

02 사람들은 청결해야 하므로 Tom은 그들에게 비누를 보내고 싶어한다.

03 그곳에는 공부해야 할 아이들이 있기 때문에 Susan은 책을 보낼 것이다.

04 그곳에는 전기가 없기 때문에 Paul은 그 지역으로 손전등을 보내고 싶어한다.

05 그곳에는 배고픈 사람들이 있으므로, Ellie는 통조림 음식을 보낼 것이다.

06 사람들은 깨끗한 물을 필요로 하므로, Sam은 그들에게 병에 든 생수를 보낼 것이다.

B

모두들 라이트 형제가 비행기를 만들었다는 것을 알고 있다. 엄밀히 말하면, 그들의 비행기는 지금의 비행기와는 같지 않다. 하지만 그들이 최초의 비행기를 만들었다는 것을 생각해 보면, 우리는 그들에게 고마워해야 한다. 어렸을 때 그 형제들은 장난감 헬리콥터를 즐겨 가지고 놀았다. 밖에 있을 때면 그들은 높이 나는 연을 날렸다. 돈을 벌기 위해 인쇄 회사를 시작했음에도 불구하고 그들은 비행에 관해 절대 잊지 않았다. 여가 시간이 생길 때마다 그들은 과거의 발명품을 연구했다. 날씨가 좋으면 형제들은 항상 밖으로 나가서 실험을 했다. 마침내 비행기를 만든 첫 번째 사람들이 되어서 그들은 1903년의 어느 역사적인 날, 수제 제작한 비행기를 날렸다.

Actual Test  p.75

1 ④ **2** ③ **3** ④ **4** ④ **5** ④ **6** ② **7** ①
8 Being tired **9** There being a tall tower
10 There being fun stories

---

1 분사구문의 주어와 주절의 주어가 다르므로 분사구문 앞에 the weather를 쓴다.

2 '손이 서로 잡혀 있었다'는 수동의 의미가 되어야 하므로 p.p.를 쓴다.

3 비인칭독립분사구문 Generally speaking(일반적으로 말하면)이 되어야 한다.

4 (A)는 주절의 주어와 분사구문의 주어가 같으므로 빈칸에 분사 Being이 오며, (B)는 주절의 주어와 분사구문의 주어가 다르므로, 날씨를 나타낼 때 쓰는 비인칭주어 It을 분사구문의 주어로 표시해야 한다.

5 After fixing은 분사구문 앞에 접속사가 온 형태이다.

6 '눈물이 얼굴에 흘러내리면서'의 의미로 「with + 목적어 + -ing」를 쓸 수 있다. fell은 falling이 되어야 옳다.

7 날씨를 나타낼 때 쓰는 가주어 It이 와서 It snowing이 되어야 한다.

8 접속사와 주어 Because I를 지우고 be동사 was를 분사 Being으로 바꾼다.

9 접속사 As를 지우고, 주절의 주어와 다르므로 There를 남겨둔 후, is를 being으로 바꾼다.

10 동사 is를 분사구문의 형태인 being으로 바꾼다.

Review Test
pp.76-78

01 ③　**02** ⑤　**03** ③　**04** ②　**05** ③　**06** ⑤
07 ③　**08** ①　**09** ④　**10** ③　**11** ⑤　**12** ⑤
13 ②　**14** ②　**15** ④　**16** ⑤　**17** ⑤　**18** ①
19 I talked to you　**20** he didn't want to hurt her feelings　**21** ③ → kicking it

01 '공부를 열심히 하지 않으면' 라는 의미로 빈칸에는 분사구문이 들어간다. 앞에 not이 있어 부정형이 된다.

02 '정상이 눈으로 덮인 채' 라는 수동의 의미를 나타내는 과거분사가 들어가야 한다.

03 considering (that)은 '~를 고려하면' 이라는 의미의 비인칭독립분사구문이다.

04 '지하철을 탔을 때' 만났다는 의미이므로 시간을 나타내는 접속사 「when＋분사」가 오는 것이 알맞다.

05 '비누가 미끄러워서' 떨어뜨렸다는 의미로 분사구문을 쓴다. 주절의 주어가 I로 분사구문의 주어와 다르므로 The soap ~이 되어야 한다.

06 '날씨가 너무 더워서' 라는 의미로 ⑤는 It being이 되어야 한다.

07 ③은 '어두워서' 라는 의미로 명암을 나타내는 비인칭주어 It을 써서 It being dark가 되어야 한다.

08 부사절을 분사구문으로 바꿀 수 있으며, 주절의 주어와 종속절의 주어가 다르므로 Jean을 남겨두고, 동사를 loving으로 고쳐야 한다.

09 주절의 주어와 같으므로 (Lisa = she) 주어는 없애고, 동사를 having으로 고친 후, 부정어는 분사구문 앞에 써준다.

10 다리가 '꼬여 있다' 는 수동의 의미를 나타내므로 빈칸에는 과거분사가 들어간다.

11 strictly speaking은 '엄밀히 말해서' 라는 의미의 비인칭독립분사구문이다.

12 '차를 살 능력이 안 돼' 라는 뜻의 분사구문이므로 be동사의 분사 형태인 Being이 들어가야 한다.

13 ②는 날씨를 나타내는 비인칭주어를 써서 It being foggy의 형태가 되어야 한다.

14 (A)는 문맥상 주절의 주어와 종속절의 주어가 같으므로 Being이 되며, (B)는 머리카락을 빨갛게 '물들인 채' 라는 수동의 의미이므로 p.p.형인 dyed가 되어야 한다.

15 (A)는 문맥상 자러 가기 '전에' 라는 의미로 접속사 before가 오며, (B)는 '~하는 동안' 이라는 의미로 while이 들어간다.

16 특정일을 나타내는 비인칭주어 It을 분사구문 앞에 써주어야 한다.

17 considering (that)은 '~을 고려하면' 이라는 의미의 비인칭독립분사구문이다.

18 분사구문에서 부정어는 분사구문 앞에 온다.

19 주절의 주어와 분사구문의 주어가 같으므로 I를 쓰고, 주절의 시제가 과거이므로 동사도 과거형인 talked가 된다.

20 주절의 주어와 종속절의 주어가 같으므로 he를 쓰고, 분사구문 앞에 부정어가 있으므로 과거시제 부정형인 didn't want로 써 준다.

21 '공을 발로 세게 차서' 라는 능동의 의미이므로 ③은 kicking it이 되어야 한다.

CHAPTER VI 수동태

UNIT **14** | 수동태의 용법   p.80

해석 세계 곳곳에서 영어가 쓰인다.

그것은 비지니스, 연구 등 다양한 목적을 위해 사용된다.

🗨 Check up 1   p.81

A 01 serve 02 was handed 03 were killed
04 explained 05 wasn't drawn
06 destroyed 07 was built 08 was told
09 were made 10 was not delivered

B 01 was received by 02 was performed by
03 is grown 04 was pulled by 05 was
turned off 06 was sold 07 was sent to me
08 was surrounded by 09 was not invited
10 to wash

A

01 웨이트리스와 웨이터는 손님에게 서빙을 한다.

02 Ann은 식당에서 메뉴를 건네 받았다.

03 자동차 사고로, 그의 부모님이 둘 다 돌아가셨다.

04 선생님은 학생들에게 수업 내용을 설명했다.

05 그 그림은 우리 오빠에 의해 그려진 게 아니야.

06 허리케인은 하루 만에 그 작은 마을을 파괴했다.

07 새로운 건물은 일주일 전에 지어졌다.

08 나는 아침 8시 30분까지 여기로 오라고 들었다.

09 이 신발과 바지는 중국에서 만들어졌다.

10 우편물은 오늘 오전에 배달되지 않았다.

> **해설** 01 능동 02 수동 (과거) 03 수동 (과거) 04 능동
> 05 수동 (과거) 06 능동 07 수동 (과거) 08 수동 (과거)
> 09 수동 (과거) 10 수동 (과거/부정형)

B

01 그 메시지는 당신 사무실에 있는 Tom에게 수신되었습니다.

02 뮤지컬은 단 세 명의 여배우들에 의해 공연되었다.

03 동아시아에서 쌀이 많이 재배된다.

04 농부의 짐마차는 말 두 마리의 말이 끈다.

05 그 휴대폰은 꺼졌다.

06 저 책은 많은 나라에서 품절되었다.

07 청구서는 월말에 나에게 보내진다.

08 그 군대는 한 시간 전에 적에게 포위당했다.

09 Ken은 네 파티에 초대받지 않았어.

10 나는 개를 목욕시키게 되었다.

> **해설** 01-06 be동사＋p.p. 07 4형식의 수동태
> 08 be동사＋p.p. 09 be동사＋not＋p.p. 10 5형식의
> 수동태: be made＋to부정사

🗨 Check up 2   p.82

A 01 are cleaned 02 needs 03 cleans
04 are used 05 is helped 06 gives
07 is not wiped 08 is made to clean

B 01 are raised 02 are dressed 03 is
bought 04 cheer 05 are protected
06 are guided 07 are trained 08 avoid

A

01 창문은 인호에 의해 청소된다.

02 인호는 창문 청소를 위해 유리창 세정제가 필요하다.

03 수미는 칠판 지우개로 칠판을 청소한다.

04 바닥을 청소하는 데 대걸레와 바구니가 사용된다.

05 보라는 바닥을 청소하는 데 Sam의 도움을 받는다.

06 Sam은 바닥을 청소하는 데 보라를 도와주었다.

07 칠판은 Sam에 의해 닦여지지 않는다. 그는 책상을 맡
고 있다.

08 보라는 교실 바닥을 청소하게 된다.

> **해설** 01 수동 02 능동 03 능동 04 수동 05 수동
> 06 능동 07 수동 08 수동 (5형식 사역동사)

B

사람과 애완동물은 특별한 관계를 맺는다. 많은 종류의 동물들이 사람에 의해 가정에서 길러진다. 이 동물에게는 형형색색의 옷이 입혀지고, 그들을 먹이기 위해 비싼 음식이 구매된다. 한편, 애완동물도 사람을 여러 방면으로 돕는다. 예를 들어 애완동물은 아프거나 혼자 사는 사람들에게 힘을 준다. 사람들과 그들의 가정은 큰 개에 의해 보호 받는다. 또한 시각장애자들은 안내견에 의해 인도를 받는다. 이 개는 위험한 상황을 감지하면 정지하도록 훈련되었다. 그 개들은 낮은 가지나 다른 장애물도 피한다.

> 해설 01 수동 02 수동 03 수동 04 능동 05 수동
> 06 수동 07 수동 08 능동

Actual Test p.83

1 ④ 2 ⑤ 3 ④ 4 ⑤ 5 ② 6 ⑤ 7 ④

8 English is spoken (by people) in many countries. 9 Some ice cream was bought for us by our teacher. [We were bought some ice cream by our teacher.] 10 His friends were seen to head toward the beach.

1 에디슨에 의해 과거에 '발명된' 것이므로 과거시제 수동태를 쓴다.

2 사역동사 make를 수동태로 바꾸면 「be made + to부정사」의 형태가 된다.

3 지각동사 hear를 수동태로 바꾸면 「be heard + to부정사」의 형태가 되므로 sing은 to sing이 된다.

4 4형식 동사 sent를 수동태로 바꾸면 「be sent to + 간접목적어」의 형태가 된다.

5 비행기가 '조종되는' 것이므로 ②의 flying은 수동태의 과거분사형 flown이 되어야 한다.

6 그가 '고용되는' 것이므로 ⑤의 hiring은 수동태의 과거분사형 hired가 되어야 한다.

7 시계가 '발견된' 것이므로 found는 수동태인 was found가 되어야 한다.

8 목적어 English를 주어로 하여 현재시제 수동태인 is spoken으로 쓴다.

9 직접목적어 some ice cream을 주어 자리로 하고, 과거시제 수동태인 was bought으로 쓴다. 동사 buy는 3형식 문장에서 전치사 for와 함께 쓰므로 for us가 된다.

10 지각동사 see의 수동태는 「be seen + to부정사」 형태로 쓴다.

UNIT 15 | 주의해야 할 수동태 p.84

해석 A: 뉴스에서 뭐라고 하니?

B: 새 올림픽 경기장이 다음 달에 완공될 거래.

Check up 1 p.85

A 01 being prepared 02 be suggested
03 had not been cleaned 04 have been imported 05 has been painted 06 be erased 07 have been stolen 08 being interviewed 09 being developed 10 have been called

B 01 died[was dead] 02 o 03 has 04 o
05 suit 06 resembles my mother 07 will happen 08 Does the snack taste 09 o 10 o

A

01 보고서는 Mr. Lee에 의해 준비되고 있다.

02 새로운 아이디어는 누구에 의해서도 제안될 수 있다.

03 그때 방은 치워지지 않았었다.

04 이 올리브 오일은 그리스에서 수입되었을 것이다.

05 교회의 천정은 유명한 화가에 의해 칠해졌다.

06 칠판은 매 수업이 끝난 후, 지워져야 한다.

07 내 지갑은 지하철에서 도난 당한 게 틀림없어.

08 네가 전화했을 때 나는 매니저에게 면접을 받고 있었어.

09 새로운 스마트폰이 그 회사에서 개발 중인 거니?

10 Ann은 그 회의에 불려갔던 게 틀림없어.

> 해설 01 현재진행 수동태 02 조동사 + be p.p. 03 과거완료 수동태 (부정형) 04 현재완료 수동태 05 현재완료 수동태 06 조동사 + be p.p. 07 조동사의 과거 + 수동태 08 과거진행형 수동태 09 현재진행형 수동태 (의문문) 10 조동사의 과거 + 수동태

B

01 그 큰 나무는 물 부족으로 죽었다.

02 그 여행 책은 시장에서 잘 팔린다.

03 나는 James가 가장 재미있는 만화책을 갖고 있는 것 같아.

04 모래는 해변에서 씻겨져 갔다.

05 이 청바지는 너에게 잘 어울려.

06 내 조카는 우리 엄마를 닮았다.

07 내일은 무언가 안 좋은 일이 일어날 것만 같아.

08 그 스낵은 달콤하니?

09 아프리카는 물이 많이 부족하다.

10 문이 제대로 닫히지 않아서, 나는 열 수가 없었다.

Check up 2
p.86

A 01 been broken 02 can be sent
03 cannot be fixed 04 should be cleaned
05 be cleaned, be planted 06 can be built

B 01 has been told 02 has been described
03 is located 04 was built 05 must have been designed 06 is considered 07 was being built 08 had been used

A

01 세탁기는 내 실수로 부서졌을 것이다.

02 세탁기는 서비스 센터로 보내질 수 있다.

03 세탁기는 센터에서 수리될 수 없다.

04 더러운 뒷마당은 우리 가족 모두에 의해 청소되어야 한다.

05 뒷마당은 이번 일요일에 청소될 것이며, 새로운 꽃들이 심어질 것이다.

06 우리 개를 위한 새로운 개 집은 아버지에 의해 지어질 수 있다.

B

여러 사람들에 의해 이야기되어져 여러분은 타지마할에 대해 알고 있을 것입니다. 타지마할은 세계에서 가장 아름다운 건축물로 묘사되어 왔습니다. 그것은 인도의 아그라에 위치해 있으며, 300년 전에 지어졌습니다. 하지만 누가 그것을 설계했는지는 확실치 않습니다. 그 건축물은 여러 터키 건축가들에 의해 설계된 것이 틀림없지만, 일반적으로 Lahauri가 책임 건축가였을 거라고 여겨집니다. 그 무덤이 지어지는 동안, 완공하기 위해 약 2만 명의 노동자와 20년의 시간이 소요되었습니다.

Actual Test
p.87

1 ③ 2 ① 3 ① 4 ⑤ 5 ② 6 ⑤ 7 ②
8 This poem must have been written in 19th century. 9 Skiing has been loved by many people. 10 The goods at these big supermarkets sell well.

1 「조동사 + be p.p.」의 형태로 쓰여야 한다.

2 동사 happen은 자동사이며 수동태로 만들 수 없다.

3 '책이 대출되었다' 는 의미의 과거완료 수동태로 바뀌어야 한다.

4 '벌을 받았어야 했다' 는 의미로 「should + have been p.p.」의 형태로 쓰여야 한다.

5 아빠에 의해 '세탁되는' 것이므로 ②는 must have been done이 되어야 한다.

6 누군가에 의해 고장이 나는 것이므로 ⑤는 수동태인 has been broken이 되어야 한다.

7 현재 '지어지는 중' 이므로 ②는 현재진행형 수동태인 being built가 되어야 한다.

8 조동사의 과거형과 수동태가 결합되어 「must + have been p.p.」의 형태가 된다.

9 현재완료 수동태인 「has + been p.p.」의 형태가 된다.

10 동사 sell은 수동의 의미가 포함된 자동사로, 수동태로 만들지 않는다.

Review Test
pp.88–90

01 ⑤ 02 ② 03 ④ 04 ④ 05 ① 06 ②
07 ⑤ 08 ③ 09 ⑤ 10 ② 11 ② 12 ⑤
13 ③ 14 ③ 15 ④ 16 ⑤ 17 ④ 18 ③
19 had been discovered 20 the game being

won **21** can be guided **22** naming →
named **23** had been playing → had been
played **24** ⑤ **25** The model was picked for
the first prize by his teacher.

---

01 뒤에 by Jack이 온 것으로 보아, 빈칸의 동사는 수동태가 되어야 한다.

02 지각동사 see의 수동태는 「be seen + to부정사」로 쓴다.

03 「조동사의 과거형 + 수동태」로 should have been p.p.의 형태가 되어야 한다.

04 동사 suit는 수동의 의미가 포함되어 수동태로 쓰지 않는 타동사이다.

05 동사 resemble은 수동태로 쓰지 않는 타동사이다.

06 지각동사의 수동태는 뒤에 to부정사가 오며, 동사 sell은 수동태의 의미가 포함된 자동사이다.

07 (A)에는 「조동사 + 수동태」의 형태로 빈칸에는 과거분사형이 오며, (B)는 사역동사의 수동태로 「be made + to 부정사」의 형태가 되어야 한다.

08 동사 happen은 자동사이며 수동태로 쓰지 않으므로 happened가 되어야 한다.

09 전화는 '발견되는' 것으로 ⑤는 수동태인 was not found가 되어야 한다.

10 「cannot + be p.p.」로 쓰여야 한다.

11 동사 lock은 수동태의 의미가 포함된 자동사이다. 주어가 3인칭 단수이므로 locks가 된다.

12 뒤에 by her가 온 것으로 보아, 수동태가 와야 하며 「has been p.p.」는 현재완료 수동태이다.

13 5형식 문장을 수동태로 바꿀 때는 목적어만 주어 자리에 올 수 있으므로 ③은 He was thought to be a real leader by me.가 되어야 한다.

14 목적어 Sarah가 주어가 되면 동사는 수동태로 「be + p.p.」 형태가 되며, 시제는 과거이다.

15 4형식 문장의 간접목적어가 주어자리에 쓰여 동사는 수동태인 「be + p.p.」 형태가 되며, 시제는 과거이다.

16 수동의 의미이므로 동사는 was handed의 수동태가 되어야 한다.

17 수동의 의미이므로 동사는 will be sent로 수동태가 되어야 한다.

18 「조동사 + be p.p.」에서 의문문이므로 조동사 can이 문두에 온다.

19 과거완료 수동태는 「had + been p.p.」의 형태로 쓴다.

20 현재진행형 수동태는 「is + being p.p.」의 형태로 쓴다.

21 조동사를 포함한 수동태는 「조동사 + be p.p.」의 형태로 쓴다.

22 물고기의 이름은 '붙여지는' 것이므로 수동태인 were newly named가 되어야 한다.

23 게임은 사람에 의해 '행해지는' 것이므로 수동태인 been played가 되어야 한다.

24 '몇 주가 소요되는' 것이므로 ④는 수동태인 were spent가 되어야 한다.

25 모형이 '뽑혔다' 는 수동의 의미이므로 was picked로 수동태가 되어야 한다.